Reach Your Po[illegible]al

SAGIT[illegible]US

Teresa Moorey

A catalogue record for this title is available from The British Library

ISBN 0 340 69717 2

First published 1998
Impression number 10 9 8 7 6 5 4 3 2 1
Year 2002 2001 2000 1999 1998

Typeset by Transet Limited, Coventry, England.
Printed in Great Britain for Hodder & Stoughton Educational, a division of Hodder Headline plc, 338 Euston Road, London NW1 3BH by Cox and Wyman, Reading, Berks.

Contents

Introduction

A PERSPECTIVE OF ASTROLOGY

Interest in the mystery and significance of the heavens is perhaps as old as humanity. If we can cast our imaginations back, to a time when there were no street lamps, televisions or even books, if we can picture how it must have been to have nothing to do through the deep nights of winter other than to sit and weave stories by the fire at the cave mouth, then we can come close to sensing how important the great dome of stars must have seemed in ancient times.

We are prone to believe that we are wiser today, having progressed beyond old superstitions. We know that all stars are like our Sun – giant nuclear reactors. We know that the planets are lumps of rock reflecting sunlight, they are not gods or demons. But how wise are we in truth? Our growing accumulation of facts brings us no closer to discovering the real meaning behind life. It may well be that our cave-dwelling ancestors knew better than us the meaning of holism. The study of astrology may be part of a journey towards a more holistic perception, taking us, as it does, through the fertile, and often uncharted realms of our own personality.

Until the seventeenth century astrology (which searches for the meaning of heavenly patterns) and astronomy (which seeks to clarify facts about the skies) were one, and it was the search for meanings, not facts that inspired the earliest investigations. Lunar phases have been found carved on bone and stone figures from as early as 15,000BCE (Before Common Era). Astrology then evolved through the civilisations of Mesopotamia and Greece among others.

Through the 'dark ages' much astrological lore was preserved in Islamic countries, but in the fifteenth century astrology grew in popularity in the West. Queen Elizabeth I had her own personal astrologer, John Dee, and such fathers of modern astronomy as Kepler and Galileo served as court astrologers in Europe.

Astrology was taught at the University of Salamanca until 1776. What is rarely appreciated is that some of our greatest scientists, notably Newton and even Einstein, were led to their discoveries by intuition. Newton was a true mystic, and it was the search for meaning – the same motivation that inspired the Palaeolithic observer – that gave rise to some of our most brilliant advances. Indeed Newton is widely believed to have been an astrologer. The astronomer Halley, who discovered the famous comet, is reported to have criticised Newton for this, whereupon Sir Isaac replied 'I have studied it Sir, you have not!'

During the twentieth century astrology enjoyed a revival, and in 1948 The Faculty of Astrological Studies was founded, offering tuition of high quality and an examination system. The great psychological Carl Jung was a supporter of astrology, and his work has expanded ideas about the mythic connections of the birth chart. Astrology is still eyed askance by many people, and there is not doubt that there is little purely scientific corroboration for astrology – the exception to this is the exhaustive statistical work undertaken by the Gauquelins. Michel Gauquelin was a French statistician whose research shows undeniable connection between professional prominance and the position of planets at birth. Now that the concept of a mechanical universe is being superseded, there is a greater chance that astrology and astronomy will reunite.

Anyone who consults a good astrologer comes away deeply impressed by the insight of the birth chart. Often it is possible to see very deeply into the personality and to be able to throw light on current dilemmas.

It is noteworthy that even the most sceptical of people tend to know their Sun sign and the characteristics associated with it.

WHAT IS A BIRTH CHART?

Your birth chart is a map of the heavens drawn up for the time, date and place of your birth. An astrologer will prefer you to be as accurate as you can about the time of day, for that affects the sign rising on the eastern horizon. This 'rising sign' is very important to your personality. However, if you do not know your birth time a chart can still be compiled for you. There will be some details missing, but useful interpretations may still be made. It is far better for the astrologer to know that your birth time is in question than to operate from a position of false certainty. The birth chart for Uri Geller, (page 4) is a simplified chart. Additional factors would be entered on the chart and considered by an astrologer, such as angles (aspects) between the planets, and the houses.

The birth chart shows each of the planets and the Moon in the astrological signs, and can be thought of as an 'energy map' of the different forces operating within the psyche. Thus the Sun sign (often called 'birth sign' or 'star sign') refers only to the position of the Sun. If the planets are in very different signs from the Sun sign, the interpretation will be greatly modified. Thus, if a person has Sun in Leo yet is somewhat introverted or quiet, this may be because the Moon was in reserved Capricorn when that person was born. Nonetheless, the Sun represents the light of consciousness, the integrating force, and most people recognise that they are typical of their Sun sign, although in some people it will be more noticeable than in others. The planets Mercury and Venus are very close to the Sun and often occupy the same sign, so intensifying the Sun-sign influence.

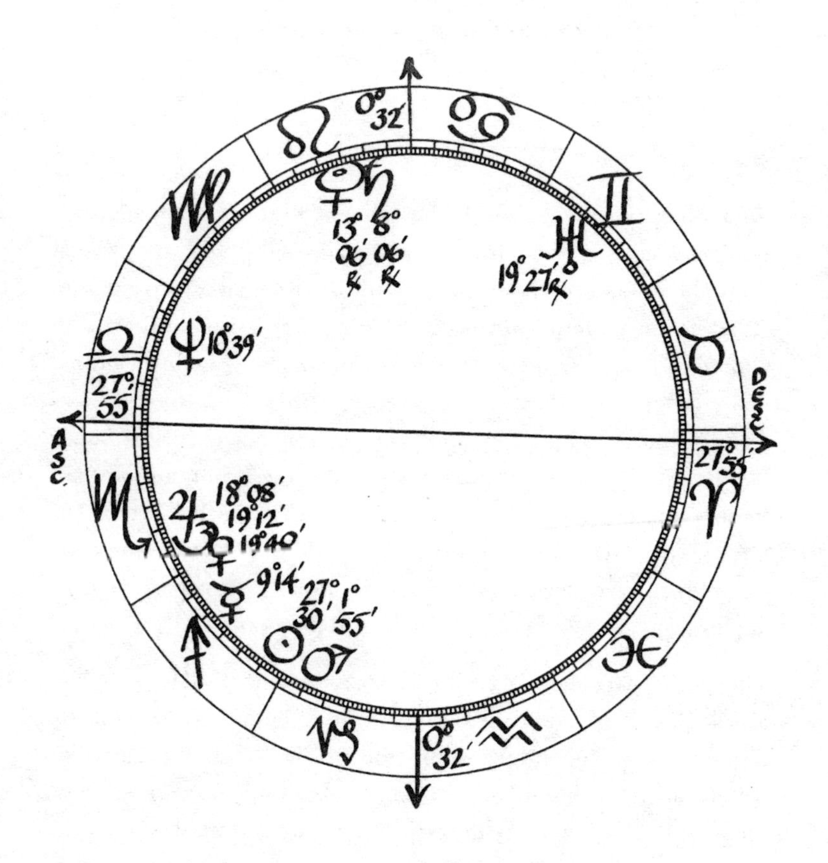

The birth chart of Uri Geller, psychic and 'spoon bender'
With Sun ☉ and Mercury ☿ in Sagittarius ♐ Uri is intent on extending the bounds of the 'possible'.

This book is written about your Sun sign, because the Sun sign serves as an accessible starting point for those wishing to learn about themselves through astrology. However, do not let your interest stop there. If you find anything helpful in comments and advice stemming from Sun sign alone, you will find your true birth chart even more revealing. The address of the Faculty of Astrological Studies appears in 'Further Reading and Resources' at the back of this book, and it is a good idea to approach them for a list of trained astrologers who can help you. Moon *phase* at birth (as distinct from Moon sign) is also very important. *The Moon and You for Beginners* (see 'Further Reading') explains this fascinating area clearly, and provides a simple chart for you to look up your Moon phase, and learn what this means for your personality.

The **planets** are life principles, energy centres. To enable you to understand the birth chart, here are their glyphs:

Sun	☉	Jupiter	♃
Moon	☽	Saturn	♄
Mercury	☿	Uranus	♅
Venus	♀	Neptune	♆
Mars	♂	Pluto	♇ (♇)

Rising Sign or **Ascendant** (**ASC**) is the way we have of meeting the world, our outward persona. **Midheaven** (**MC**) refers to our image, aspirations, how we like to be seen.

The **signs** are modes of expression, ways of being. Here are their glyphs:

Aries	♈	Libra	♎
Taurus	♉	Scorpio	♏
Gemini	♊	Sagittarius	♐
Cancer	♋	Capricorn	♑
Leo	♌	Aquarius	♒
Virgo	♍	Pisces	♓

Using knowledge of the glyphs you can see that the Sun is in Sagittarius in our example birth chart (page 4).

HOW DOES ASTROLOGY WORK?

We cannot explain astrology by the usual methods of cause and effect. In fact, there are many things we cannot explain. No one can define exactly what life is. We do not know exactly what electricity is, but we know how to use it. Few of us have any idea how a television set works, but we know how to turn it on. Although we are not able to explain astrology we are still able to use it, as any capable astrologer will demonstrate.

Jung discovered something called 'synchronicity'. This he defined as 'an acausal connecting principle'. Simply, this means that some events have a meaningful connection *other than cause and effect.* The planets do not cause us to do things, but their movements are synchronistic with our lives. The old dictum 'as above, so below' applies here. It is a mystery. We can't explain it, but that doesn't mean we should refuse to believe in it. A little boy on a visit to the circus saw an elephant for the first time and said 'There's no such thing'. We may laugh at the little boy, but how many of us respond to things we do not understand in this way?

The planetary positions in your birth chart are synchronistic with the time of your birth, when you took on separate existence, and they are synchronistic with your individuality in this life. They have much to say about you.

MYTH AND PSYCHOLOGY

The planets are named after the old gods and goddesses of Rome, which in turn link in with Greek and other pantheons. The planets represent 'life principles' – forces that drive the personality, and as such they can be termed 'archetypal'. This means that they are basic ideas, universal within human society and are also relevant in terms of the forces that, in some inexplicable way, inhabit the corners of the universe and inform the Earth and all human institutions. Thus the assertive energy that is represented by Mars means energetic action of all sorts – explosions and fires, wars, fierce debates and personal anger. Put briefly, here are the meanings of the planets:

- Mercury – intellect and communication
- Venus – love, unifying, relating
- Mars – assertion, energy, fighting spirit
- Jupiter – expansion, confidence, optimism
- Saturn – limitation, discipline
- Uranus – rebellion, independence
- Neptune – power to seek the ideal, sense the unseen
- Pluto – power to transform and evolve

These principles are modified according to the astrological sign they inhabit; thus Venus in Pisces may be gently loving, dreamy and self-sacrificing, while Venus in Aries will be demanding and adventurous in relationships. Thus the planets in signs form a complex psychological framework – and that is only part of the story of chart interpretation!

In the old mythologies these 'energies' or 'archetypes' or 'gods' were involved in classical dramas. An example is the story of Saturn and Uranus. Uranus is the rejecting father of Saturn, who later castrates and murders his father – thus innovative people reject reactionaries, who then murder them, so the revolutionary part of the personality is continually 'killed off' by the restrictive part. The exact positions and angles between the planets will indicate how this and other myths may come to life. In addition, the mere placement of planets by sign – and, of course, especially the Sun sign, call forth various myths as illustrations. The ancient myths are good yarns but they are inspired and vivid dramatisations of what may be going on repeatedly within your personality and that of your nearest and dearest. Myths are used by many modern psychologists and therapists in a tradition that has grown since Jung. We shall be using mythic themes to illustrate internal dynamics in this book.

SIGN	QUALITY	ELEMENT
Aries	Cardinal	Fire
Taurus	Fixed	Earth
Gemini	Mutable	Air
Cancer	Cardinal	Water
Leo	Fixed	Fire
Virgo	Mutable	Earth
Libra	Cardinal	Air
Scorpio	Fixed	Water
Sagittarius	Mutable	Fire
Capricorn	Cardinal	Earth
Aquarius	Fixed	Air
Pisces	Mutable	Water

THE SIGNS OF THE ZODIAC

There are twelve signs, and each of these belongs to an Element – Earth, Fire, Air or Water, and a Quality – Cardinal, Fixed or Mutable. The Cardinal signs are more geared to action, the Fixed tend to remain stable and rooted, whereas the Mutable signs are adaptable, changeable.

Jung defined four functions of consciousness – four different ways of perceiving the world – 'thinking', 'feeling', 'sensation' and 'intuition'. Thinking is the logical, evaluative approach that works in terms of the mind. Feeling is also evaluative, but this time in relation to culture and family needs. This is not the same as emotion, although 'feeling' people often process emotions more smoothly than other types. Jung saw 'feeling' as rational, too. 'Sensation' refers to the 'here and now', the five physical senses, while 'intuition' relates to the possible, to visions and hunches. Jung taught that we tend to have one function uppermost in consciousness, another one or maybe two secondary and another repressed or 'inferior', although we all possess each of these functions to some degree.

Jungian ideas are being refined and expanded, and they are incorporated into modern methods of personality testing, as in the Myers-Briggs test. If a prospective employer has recently given you such a test, it was to establish your talents and potential for the job. However, the basic four-fold division is still extremely useful, and I find that it is often of great help in assisting clients to understand themselves, and their partners, in greater depth – for we are all apt to assume that everyone processes information and applies it in the same way as we do. But they don't! It is worthy of mention that the important categories of 'introverted' and 'extraverted' were also identified by Jung. In astrology, Fire and Air signs seems to be extraverted, generally speaking, and Earth and Water introverted – and this has been borne out by the statistical research of the astrologer, Jeff Mayo. However, this doesn't mean that all feeling and sensation people are introverted and all intuitive and thinkers extraverted – this is definitely not the case, and calls for more detailed examination of the chart (e.g. lots of Fire and Water may mean an extravert feeling type).

Very broadly speaking we may link the Fire signs to intuition, Water to feeling, Earth to sensation and Air to thinking. Often thinking and feeling are drawn together and sensation and intuition are attracted, because they are opposites. This probably happens because we all seek to become more whole, but the process can be painful. The notion of the four functions, when understood, does help to throw light on some of the stumbling blocks we often encounter in relationships. However, some people just do not seem to fit. Also Fire doesn't always correspond to intuition, Water to feeling, etc. – it seems this is usually the case, but not all astrologers agree. Some link Fire with feeling, Water with intuition, and most agree that other chart factors are also important. As with all theories, this can be used to help, expand and clarify, not as a rigid system to impose definitions. We shall be learning more about these matters in relation to the Sun sign in the following pages.

THE PRECESSION OF THE EQUINOXES

One criticism often levelled at astrology is that 'the stars have moved' and so the old signs are invalid. There is some truth in this, and it is due to a phenomenon called 'The Precession of the Equinoxes'. The beginning of the sign Aries occurs when the Sun is overhead at the equator, moving northwards. This is called the Spring Equinox, for now day and night are equal all over the globe, and the first point of Aries is called the 'equinoctial point'. Because the Earth not only turns on its axis but 'rocks' on it (imagine a giant knitting needle driven through the poles – the Earth spins on this, but the head of the needle also slowly describes a circle in space) the 'equinoctial point' has moved against the background of stars. Thus, when the Sun is overhead at the equator, entering Aries, it is no longer at the start of the constellation of Aries, where it occurred when the signs were named, but is now in the constellation of Pisces. The 'equinoctial point' is moving backwards into Aquarius, hence the idea of the dawning 'Aquarian age'.

So where does that leave astrology? Exactly in the same place, in actuality. For it all depends on how you think the constellations came to be named in the first place. Did our ancestors simply look up and see the shape of a Ram in the sky? Or did they – being much more intuitive and in tune with their surroundings than we are – feeling sharply aware of the quality, the energies around at a certain time of the year, and *then* look skywards, translating what they sensed into a suitable starry symbol? This seems much more likely – and you have only to look at the star groups to see that it takes a fair bit of imagination to equate most of them with the figures they represent! The Precession of the Equinoxes does not affect astrological interpretation, for it is based upon observation and intuition, rather than 'animals in the sky'.

USING THIS BOOK

Reach Your Potential – Sagittarius explores your Sun sign and what this means in terms of your personality; the emphasis is on self-exploration. All the way through, hints are given to help you to begin to understand yourself better, ask questions about yourself and use what you have to maximum effect. This book will show you how to use positive Sagittarian traits to your best advantage, and how to neutralise negative Sagittarian traits. Don't forget that by reading it you are consenting, however obliquely, to the notion that you are connected in strange and mysterious ways to the web of the cosmos. What happens within you is part of a meaningful pattern that you can explore and become conscious of, thereby acquiring greater influence on the course of your life. Let this encourage you to ask further questions.

Some famous Sagittarians

William Blake, Chris Evert, Uri Geller, Magaret Mead, Emily Dickinson, Christina Rosetti, Toulouse Lautrec, Hector Berlioz, Beethoven, Maria Callas, Andrew Carnegie, Edith Cavell, Winston Churchill, Noel Coward, Sammy Davis Jnr, Joe DiMaggio, Walt Disney, Betty Grable, Grimaldi, John Milton, Lee Remick, Lillian Russell, Frank Sinatra, Mark Twain, Edith Piaf, Jimi Hendrix.

Naturally, the boundless optimism, enthusiasm and expansive nature of Sagittarius can be an asset to those in public life or the arts.

Sage, Centaur or Opportunist – what sort of Sagittarius are you?

Here is a quiz to give an idea of how you are operating at the moment. Its tone is light-hearted, but the intent is serious and you may find out something interesting about yourself. Don't think too hard about the answers, just pick the one that appeals to you most.

1. **Your friend comes to you with sad tales about his or her love life. How are you most likely to react?**

   a) ❑ You stare abstractedly out of the window – until it dawns on you that you know the errant lover – who is extremely attractive! Then you listen with more interest, wondering if there may be a chance for you to step in . . .

   b) ❑ You try to distract your friend with bright-and-breezy pleasantries. All this misery is so boring.

   c) ❑ You do your best to show your friend the philosophical angle and to cheer him or her up by emphasising wider perspectives. Probably this lover is not for your friend.

2. **At work you choose to move to another department, but instead of this being the career move you anticipated, you find you are involved in planning large-scale redundancies – and part of your job will be to break the news. How do you react.**

   a) ❑ These people will find more jobs – you always can if you want to. There may be more scope for you to advance in this changing company.

   b) ❑ This job isn't as challenging as you hoped, but you're planning your holidays. Anyway, you've heard a new multinational is coming to your area. Or you might go abroad . . .

c) ❑ You find yourself thinking of all the ways this power could be used, and all the social implications. maybe you could set up a new company, to employ them all. You've got a few ideas . . .

3. **Your friends have moved house, to somewhere they lovingly call 'bijou'. You are asked around for a cup of tea and your opinion. You find the place with difficulty – it's about the size of a hamster cage. So you:**

   a) ❑ Say 'It won't cost much to curtain and carpet this place. Actually, I'm selling my bathroom rug, and it would go wall-to-wall in here. I don't want much for it.'

   b) ❑ Say 'Ha, needed a microscope to find you! It'll be all arms and legs hanging out of the window, won't it – like Alice in Wonderland.' You perceive their faces have fallen so you try to recuperate: 'Of course, it can be sort of fascinating and magical – a small place. That's why I mentioned Alice in Wonderland. And you'll have to watch those steep stairs, or it will be like when she fell down the . . . but never mind, old places have atmosphere. The pub next door's said to be haunted. Perhaps this is, too.'

   c) ❑ You offer them all the advice you can about extending, going imaginatively into all the possibilities – not that they ever asked!

4. **You have set your heart on a flat or house. It seems exactly 'you' – view over the hills/proximity to airport/trendiest place imaginable. But someone has put in an offer, or signed the rent contract, so you:**

   a) ❑ Go to see the agent and top the offer, whatever it takes.

   b) ❑ Convince yourself it doesn't really matter too much, and start looking for somewhere else.

c) ❑ Realise that this is for the best, which will be revealed in the future. You will let things take their course for a while.

5. **Which set of the following phrases appeals the most to you – don't think, just choose:**

   a) ❑ Give me freedom, variety, the latest and the greatest – life's a breeze, don't fence me in.

   b) ❑ Let me learn, explore, expand and experience – embrace the whole wide wonderful world.

   c) ❑ Lay out for me the carpet of history, the borders of mystery. Let me keep my soul aloft.

6. **What do you think would be your favourite holiday?**

   a) ❑ A month in a sin capital, with wine, song and members of the opposite sex.

   b) ❑ A trip to the Valley of the Kings, or to Outer Mongolia, in a Land Rover.

   c) ❑ Swimming with the dolphins, or a month in the ashram of your choice.

7. **That familiar envelope with the red print has fallen on your doormat again. How will you react?**

   a) ❑ Forget about it (if you're honest, it's too scary to contemplate).

   b) ❑ Think vaguely about selling something or getting a part-time job – you know you can cope.

   c) ❑ Take the attitude 'the universe will provide; it always has in the past'.

8. **You have been invited to a friend's party. What are you most looking forward too?**

   a) ❑ You'll probably go, for a laugh. On the other hand,

there's that other invitation . . . You'll find out who else is going and keep your options open.

b) ☐ It will be great to meet everyone and tell them about your new job/romance/trip to Sri Lanka.

c) ☐ Parties can be so superficial. You might not go. You think that date clashes with your meditation class.

9. **We all feel wonderful at the start of a new romance. What goes principally through your mind?**

a) ☐ That you'll live it up together and have a ball – and that there won't be that wretched issue of commitment and ties that has always bedevilled you in the past.

b) ☐ That this will be the most fantastic adventure ever, sexually and otherwise, with the highest of highs and no lows.

c) ☐ That you have at last found someone with the depth and scope to enter a world of magic and to take flight with you.

Now count up your score. What do you have most of – a's, b's or c's?

Mostly a's. You seem to be the 'opportunist' type of Sagittarius. You have a very positive outlook and a quick mind that looks for a way to turn every situation to your advantage, and you usually succeed. You have no time for losers, clinging vines or weeping willows. Probably you enjoy life greatly – or tell yourself you do. Are you not just a little bit careless at times? And superficial? And unreliable? The time may soon come where you seek something with more depth and meaning in life. Failing that, something may happen to show you that you are not inviolable and force you to stop and reflect. Best make the choice yourself, and seek a little philosophy from interest rather than need.

Mostly b's. You're the fairly 'average' cheerful sort of Centaur. You love to enjoy life, explore and adventure, and you have a great faith in your own abilities, for the most part. For those times when things aren't so good, you may want to explore inner space and to develop more of an instinct for how other people are feeling. And you may want a *real* adventure.

Mostly c's. You are something of a Sage. Often charitable and usually very positive, you look beyond everyday concerns and your horizons are the infinite. You are deep, imaginative and creative, and it is probable that you are indeed wise, having taken the trouble to formulate a set of spiritual values. To you life is an exciting quest. However others may not always understand you. Learn also to laugh at yourself once in a while.

If you found that in many cases none of the answers seemed anywhere near to fitting you, then it may be that you are an uncharacteristic Sagittarius. This may be because there are factors in your astrological chart that frustrate the expression of your Sun sign, or it may be because there is a preponderance of other signs, outweighing the Sagittarius part. Whatever the case may be, your Sun-sign potential needs to be realised. Perhaps you will find something to ring a few bells in the following pages.

1 The essential Sagittarius

We shall not cease from exploration
And the end of all our exploring
Will be to arrive where we started
And know the place for the first time

T. S. Eliot

BORN UNDER A WANDERING STAR

Sagittarius is the adventurer of the zodiac, whirling from place to place, encounter to encounter, idea to idea. Eternal optimists, your confidence is boundless as the horizon, and every Sagittarius just knows that if the dice roll, their number is sure to come up – if not this time, then the next. Your quick wit can get you out of a dodgy situation or turn it to your advantage in a twinkling.

This is a flamboyant sign, and when describing you there can be a tendency to resort to overblown phrases. Yes, you are excessive, ebullient, with eight-cylinder personalities running at full throttle, *but* – and this is a very big 'but' – in many Sagittarians this is anything but obvious. Many Sagittarians travel only internally, on the wings of fantasy, heading for horizons of the abstract. The quiet, ordinary Sagittarius is not by any means as rare as the Dodo, and for these the merry fortune-hunter is simply a metaphor for something that is, or should be, going on somewhere inside. With this in mind, read on.

For the most part this is a sign of strong principles. You are gallant, kind to animals, a champion of the weak and good humoured. Sagittarius is no stranger to accidents, but you shrug them off, knowing that disaster is inevitably followed by happy happenstance. Sagittarius is a philosopher, in more ways than one. For the most part, this is a highly moral sign, although there is no doubt you are apt to interpret the rules very much to your own advantage on occasion. Many Sagittarians are quite sedentary. It may be hard to catch traces of the adventurer beneath their quiet exterior. In their minds, however, they are wandering beneath the stars, playing with possibilities, concepts, potentials and bringing creative imagination to bear.

SAGITTARIUS BODY LANGUAGE

Some Sagittarians are circumspect in their movements, keeping their elbows well in and their thumbs concealed in closed fists, but these are rather the exception. A strong Sagittarius predisposes to sweeping gestures and spreading posture, with legs stretched out and hands gesticulating. You may have a habit of tossing your head, and Sagittarian eyes often seem fixed on some far-off, invisible horizon. You tend to find it hard to keep still, but yours is not a nervous fidgeting but more a restless shifting that indicates you need to move on, in some way. When Sagittarius goes into action, you may be purposeful and surprisingly unobtrusive, for despite your versatility you can be very focussed at times. Also some Sagittarians are dreamers and you can sit still for ages while your mind darts from one corner of the galaxy to another. It's often the expression in your eyes that can give a clue.

MYTHS OF THE CENTAUR

The Sagittarian Centaur is unique, for it is a truly mythical beast, half man and half horse. This tells us something about the nature of Sagittarius, for while the horse body may yearn for the freedom of the plains, fired by the rampant lust of the stallion, the human head and torso is preoccupied with meanings and concepts, morals and philosophy. In addition, this centaur is also an archer. The fiery arrow is not aimed to wound but to light a path to the stars themselves. By no means all Sagittarians realise their potential for spirituality, but those who do find their 'divine discontent' is assuaged.

In ancient myth centaurs were known for the licentious habit of abducting young maidens on their wedding night. The horse is one of many goddess symbols, embodying Her power, grace and fertility. These mischievous centaurs are rather a personification of that spirit, in all women, that remains unbridled, adventurous and wild, and that retains freedom and a passionate lust for life, whatever other commitments and restraints there may be.

Many goddesses are associated with the horse, for instance Gaullish Epona, Irish Etain and Macha, Indian Samjuna, Greek Menalippe, Hippia and Hecate and Welsh Rhiannon – we will be looking more closely at Rhiannon's story later in this chapter. With its beauty, fertility, strength and speed the horse symbolises the ability to create not only the physical but also the conceptual, the spiritual. The horse is a traveller between worlds, a creature of magic and subtlety as well as brute force – and this has much to convey about Sagittarian potential.

Chiron

Perhaps the best known of Centaur myths is that of Chiron. It was Chiron who instructed Asclepius, son of Apollo and god of medicine, in the healing arts. Chiron was immortal, and although he had accidentally wounded himself with one of the poisoned arrows of Hercules, shooting himself in the foot (with Sagittarian clumsiness!), he could not die but

must live in torment, until his life was swapped for that of the saviour of mankind, Prometheus, and the centaur at last found rest. Although wild, Chiron was king of the centaurs, gentle and wise, instructing many heroes, including Achilles, in the arts of hunting, healing, philosophy and music. But while Chiron could heal others, he could never heal his own burning wound.

Here we have the archetype of the wounded healer, someone who, through his own suffering, possesses many gifts and yet can never make himself well. For Sagittarius this has significance, because for all the optimism and good cheer that the sign possesses, they still carry a 'wound'. This is the realisation that the gulf between the animal and the divine can never be bridged, and that there is a great divide between the brilliance of vision and the limitation of humanity. And yet there is a connection, a hope, a magic. There is inspiration and a sense of eternal meanings, and that is the healing gift that Sagittarius can bring to the human condition. It is both a wound and a paradox, and it is one of the factors that unites both the tragic and the comic in Sagittarius, lifting them out of the slap-dash and into the celestial, sometimes in a single leap. Of course, by no means all Sagittarians respond to these rarefied influences, but it is only when in the presence of some eternal truth that the Sagittarian wagon finally comes to rest.

ELEMENT, QUALITY, AND RULING PLANET

We have seen that each of the signs of the zodiac belongs to one of the Elements, Earth, Fire, Air or Water, and one of the Qualities, Cardinal, Fixed or Mutable. Sagittarius is Mutable Fire. Sagittarius is the most unbounded of all of the signs. Its leaping flames are uncontrollable, its fiery arrows pierce and illuminate every corner of every dimension of experience. Like a firework its energy crackles, flares and dies, to be rekindled by the next wild scheme or wonderful vision. 'Fire' in this sense is not about being hot tempered, and indeed, although Sagittarians may lose their temper in spectacular plate-flinging fashion, they are one of the most good tempered of the signs and rarely wound viciously or bear a grudge. Their 'arrows' are very much conceptual ones, and they aim high. A deeper meaning is concerned with the real nature of Fire, for this is a transformative Element, of pure energy. Flames seem almost to come from another dimension, and this tells us something about Fire-sign people in that they live in the world of the possible rather than the actual, they are vibrant with ideas and may inhabit the future, or even the past, but rarely do they live wholeheartedly in the mundane present. Fire-sign people often follow hunches, as if they can see around corners, and while most Sagittarians are quite ordinary, adapting themselves to nine-to-five jobs and trips to the supermarket, of all the signs this is the most prophetic and the most attuned to the potential, rather than the day to day.

We have also seen that the Element of Fire has some things in common with what Jung called the 'intuitive' function. This idea of intuition isn't quite the same as the 'gut feelings' that many Earth- or Water-sign people get, or the sort of idea that Air-sign people pick up on the ether. Rather it is a concept of life that projects consciousness into the future and lives by inspiration and visions. Neither is this intuition about anything airy-fairy. One thing is most unlikely – that Sagittarius is actually absorbed in any task in hand, however efficient they may be, Sagittarius is several jumps ahead, and this can make for inspiration or disaster.

Sagittarius is the ninth sign of the zodiac and third and last of the Fiery triad. First is the Fire sign of Aries, the Pioneer, next Earthy Taurus the Farmer, followed by Airy Gemini, the Communicator and Thinker. Hot on their heels follows Cancer, Water sign of Family and Clan, then Leo, Fire sign of the Monarch, and Virgo, second Earth sign, the Reaper and Sorter. Airy Libra, the Diplomat and Relater comes next and then Watery Scorpio, sign of Passion, Soul and all that is hidden. From the depths of Scorpio we shoot to the heights of Sagittarius – this use of the word 'heights' by no means indicates that Sagittarius is any way better (although Sagittarians may assert they are!). Sagittarian wisdom can be seen to complement that of Scorpio, for from the scouring of the soul we achieve our capacity to discern meanings – a Sagittarian theme.

In the Northern Hemisphere Sagittarius marks the Sun's final descent to the Midwinter Solstice, and the longest night of the year. This is interesting because in some ways no sign is more life-affirming and ablaze with energy than the Centaur. However, the approach of darkness coincides with the growth of inner wisdom, and in truth Sagittarius is most concerned with the flames of the spirit. This is also the jolliest time of the year in many parts of the globe as preparations for Christmas take over and Sagittarian bonhomie and appetite for the good things of life seem to infuse all. As we approach the solstice and the time of greatest darkness, so we also come close to the point when light again begins to grow over the winter landscape.

For those in the Southern Hemisphere, the Sun enters Sagittarius to make ascent to its highest point, the Midsummer Solstice, and so light and life are soaring towards their zenith, like the fiery arrow of the Archer. However, just as the time of greatest fulfilment is reached, so light begins to fade and we are called to look inwards once more as the Sun slowly recedes. So for the Southern Hemisphere we have the theme of darkness within light, as for the Northern we have light within darkness. Both these are equally applicable to this sign of sagacity and spiritual significance.

Each sign is said to have a 'Ruling Planet'. This means that there is a planet that has a special affinity with the sign whose energies are most at home when expressed in terms of that sign. The Ruling

Planet for Sagittarius is Jupiter, largest and brightest of the planets. Jupiter is named after the Roman king of the Olympian gods, who was also called Jove (hence 'jovial') his Greek counterpart being Zeus. Jupiter was regal and almost (but not quite) omnipotent. He dispensed justice and wisdom, but he was also profligate and self-indulgent, fathering countless children by goddesses, nymphs and humans alike, and often appearing in the guise of a variety of animals and objects, such as a swan, a bull or a shower of gold, in order to ingratiate himself into the arms and the bed of his current darling. Here Jupiter displays the generative power, the lack of restraint and the ability to shape-change that we may associate with Sagittarius.

Jupiter/Zeus vaunts male superiority in a way that is quite insufferable if we take the myths at face value. However, he also has a wife, Hera, without whose jealous attempts to thwart him his adventures would have less meaning – for what is the point of rebellion, intrigue and philandering if there are no boundaries to push back? There would be no thrill, no gamble, no danger. Hera is demoted in the Greek pantheon, and tales tell of Zeus's retaliations against her, hanging her by her hair from Heaven, as a punishment for her shrewishness. However, Hera is a most ancient and powerful Triple Goddess; she was a dignified expression of female sexuality and a daughter of the flesh and of time. In a sense she is the initiator. She it is who embodies the forces that shape the Sagittarian vision. Tempered in the cauldron of earthly limitation and its own fiery outpourings, Sagittarius really does acquire wisdom, significance and power.

POLYANNA

One of the most lovable things about you Sagittarians is your optimism, which is almost never failing. If there is a silver lining, you will find it. Mostly this makes you heartening companions. You seem to bounce back from the most appalling catastrophes, smiling as if you've just finished a ride at the fairground. Of course, like all humans, you get desperate and depressed at times, and this may seem all the more dramatic because of your usual cheerfulness, but it rarely lasts long. On other occasions you may seem naïve and quite out of step with reality and the feelings of ordinary mortals. Like Voltaire's Candide you may assert that all is for the best, in the best of all possible worlds, even for those who are about to be burnt at the stake for heresy!

Sagittarius usually means well, and for the most part your good humour is infectious. At other times this sign's indestructible self-satisfaction can be a trial. Sagittarius is one of the signs that is most agile when it comes to taking the moral high ground. However, by no means all Sagittarians resort to this and most are, above all, eager to use each and every situation to improve and expand themselves. Like Lewis Carroll's Duchess, Sagittarius believes that everything's got a moral if only you can find it, and this makes you whimsical earnest and often hilariously funny.

Because Sagittarius really believes in luck you often attract it. A Sagittarian gardener, frustrated in his attempts to grow champion turnips, may well find that the infertile soil is actually full of oil and he is sitting on several million dollars in his own back garden. Insults and sarcasm fall like paper darts from the Archer's back. Post you a poison pen letter and you'll think it's a joke. If your enemies send you a tarantula you'll assume it got separated from a gift-basket of tropical fruit, and keep the thing as a pet. There really is a lot to be said for seeing the best in everything and everyone, especially yourself. However, there are drawbacks. The most obvious one is that without a little ordinary humility no improvement is possible, and the adaptable Archer may find that conceit has hardened to such a tough chrysallis that there is no hope of a butterfly ever emerging.

Another drawback can be that relationships become difficult, if not impossible, if one is always right. Last but not least, Sagittarian jollity can become a little forced if you refuse ever to let yourself feel down, fleeing from all wounds and negative feelings into the fiction that you are 'best, in the best of all possible worlds' and repressing pain and loss to the detriment of your overall balance and health. Some Sagittarians, when they are threatened by a mood, will go absent until they have walked away their blues, which is fine as a coping mechanism consciously applied but not so good when it is a metaphor for inner escapism. A really wise Sagittarian faces all, in the true optimism of courage and ability to cope rather than the false optimism of denial.

FOOT-IN-MOUTH DISEASE

Sagittarian tactlessness is proverbial, but not universal. Many Sagittarians, especially the women, do make tremendous efforts to say the right thing and often succeed so admirably that a conversation with them leaves others looking at life with new zest. Other Sagittarians, I'm afraid, do reel from one verbal gaff to another.

However, Sagittarius is usually incapable of malice, and while you may love to tell jokes, you rarely laugh at others' expense. Genuinely, you wish to cheer them up and may be quite crestfallen if this fails. In addition you may be quite bewildered by malice directed at you as a result of your blundering. After all, you meant well. Sagittarius is frank and truthful, for 'the truth shall set you free' – although there may be some resourceful stretching of the truth at times.

In general, you are a generous person and as you stagger closer and closer to a verbal cliff, others should remind themselves that you are worth twenty false flatterers, and learn from you how to laugh and shrug their shoulders. If you are a Sagittarian, regularly finding that you have said too much, you may be telling yourself you don't care. Be honest – is this really, really true? Wouldn't you rather make people feel good? And are you truly expressing what you mean when you upset people? Take your foot out of your mouth, button your lip and count to ten. Then say something really wise and meaningful.

PROMISES, PROMISES

We all have our down side, and this is often at variance, if not totally opposite to the face we present to the world. Not that we are 'two-faced' for this concealed side is often equally obscured from ourselves, and something of which we are deeply ashamed if we are confronted by it. A sign as noble as Sagittarius sometimes has something very smelly in the basement, and it can happen that Sagittarian unreliability, which often stems from the grand impulse to try anything and not to say no to anyone, degenerates into evasiveness and even, well, meanness.

It isn't hard to see that the casual approach of the Centaur could lead to superficiality, that you may be so preoccupied with your current schemes that you become thoughtless and inconsiderate, or even that your truthfulness could decay to insincerity, when you just can't be bothered to get to grips. But that your exuberant idealism could ever be mean may come as a surprise. Of course, this isn't overt meanness, and it bears a generous face. Sagittarius will promise to lend friends money/back their business venture/take them to Egypt/marry them – and will promise this over and over again in a variety of different ways, but when the friends turn up to collect the cash, or in their glad rags for holiday or wedding, they find that something has come up and that Sagittarius is unavailable. Never mind, there's always tomorrow, or the day after, or next week, and 'you know that I'll always support you/have every confidence in your enterprise/will love you for ever and ever'.

After a while friends' faith and patience wear thin, and they confront Sagittarius with the fact you are letting them down. Some Sagittarians are affected by selective deafness at this point or seem genuinely bewildered. Others may apologise with disarming frankness and may truly intend to do better in the future. You might – or you may continue to be unreliable, as much to your own chagrin as theirs. With others the scenario is less pleasant. Unable to face what you have perpetrated, Sagittarius deftly turns the tables. Sagittarius may cite chapter and verse of incidents others cannot remember, and while they may suspect you of invention, are they really going to say 'Liar'? Resourcefully and with bare-faced cheek, Sagittarius has occupied the moral high ground. Where formerly they were merely let down, now they are treated to condescending superiority that can make them feel like dirt – a mere mortal call to account the king of the gods himself? Get back down where you belong! Not only has the promised benefit been withheld but others' self-respect has been adroitly whipped from under them too. If that isn't meanness . . . ? If they have lent you money, they can kiss it goodbye, for there will always be an excellent reason why they cannot have it back until tomorrow – and 'tomorrow' never comes. And yet if they have promised this sort of Sagittarian anything, from a cup of tea to their life's savings, you will be there, on the dot to collect – and Jupiter help them if they haven't got it, right and tight and readily available.

Of course this is, or ought to be, easy to deal with, and their best approach is to cut straight through the flannel and tell Sagittarius exactly where to get off. However, most of us have a concealed inheritance of guilt, or unconscious memories held in our bones, of when we were needy, naughty children, and Sagittarian superiority evokes this to perfection. Sagittarius carries the day and smells of roses – but there's still that whiff from the basement . . . .

As with all such situations, understanding throws a completely new light and what appears reprehensible does, in fact, merit sympathy.

For at the root of such behaviour is the Sagittarian difficulty in adapting to the constraints of ordinary life. All should be possible 'in the best of all possible worlds'. Most poignant of all, Sagittarius feels capable of honouring promises fit for the king of the gods, and when this is impossible, that moral high ground, however shaky, is the only recourse. It may be hard for more pragmatic souls to understand the pain and difficulty associated with this. Say what you mean, mean what you say, we all know there are limits, you can't do everything, we fail sometimes – all these things are true. However, to Sagittarius, accepting this at a deep level can be extremely painful and can do violence to all you hold dear – which is that world of the 'possible'. Sagittarius really wants things to be wonderful, and wants to be wonderful. Being insufferable, villainous or creating disappointment and ruin is not the Sagittarian intention – ever. Sagittarius is afraid to fail, that all the great schemes will be crushed by the material world, and that Sagittarius does not have the maturity to stick at what needs to be done. If commitments are made and adhered to, then you must face limitations, not only in the world but in yourself – and perhaps you aren't quite as 'divine' as you thought. If you are 'that sort' of Sagittarian, recognising a portrait of yourself, however exaggerated, in the above, do remember that dreams are not built in the 'real' world, or, if they are, they are never the same as the idea that gave birth to them; that there are restrictions and restraints, but not upon the soul, and that to admit some things are not possible and to be frank about one's own limitations is not an admission of defeat but a way to set the soul free.

THE GRASS IS ALWAYS GREENER . . .

We have seen that Sagittarius values the 'possible'. The trouble with the possible is that it can never be the actual, the here and now, what has been achieved, etc, etc. The land of the 'possible' is always over the next hill in the great blue yonder. Seeking the promised land in whatever form has earned Sagittarius the labels of inconsistent, unreliable, 'never finishes anything', 'always needs freedom' and similar. It is true that this sign does not always stay to reap what has been sown, but there is far more here than simple boredom.

In some form it is the Sagittarian 'mission' to push back consciousness, to explore and extend boundaries. To you it is not the destination that counts, but the journey. To many people this can seem ridiculous, as it does indeed to many Sagittarians, when it is put like that. We are all subject to the pressures of our culture, and Sagittarians may call themselves restless and discontented – you may be, but it is a divine discontent. You may feel uneasy with yourself because you are always seeking, rarely satisfied with the ordinary, although you may cope with it – you may feel you should settle down, be normal. However, the point of having visions is that it opens up the human consciousness and draws us ever onwards – and the point of dreams is not only so that we may, some day, have a dream come true, but because dreams inspire and increase our creativity. The wild-eyed prophet may seem a million miles from that cheery, inconsequential Sagittarius others have come to know and love, and equally far from the thoughtful Sagittarius, with interests in poetry or philosophy, or the sporting, fast-driving, slap-you-on-the-back Sagittarius, or the active Sagittarius who organises jumble sales, runs a company, a family and a large vegetable garden and still has time to drive friends to the shops – or just that commonplace Sagittarius who does nothing much but has a roguish grin and a far-away look sometimes. However, somewhere inside every Sagittarius is a longing to push back the fences and explore, mentally or physically. If this is you, give yourself permission to be 'different' if that is what it takes. 'Seek, and ye shall find,' and then seek some more. You will find many a kindred spirit on your journey.

THE STORY OF RHIANNON

Welsh myth tells of Rhiannon, a goddess who married a mortal man and thus found at length that she had become, very literally, a horse to carry burdens upon her back. Some people say that Rhiannon is the goddess of love and the ancient earth goddess herself, and that her humiliation tells a tale of how the Goddess became estranged from the hearts and the worship of humans. However, here we may just discern some themes that are relevant for Sagittarius.

After her marriage to the human king Pwyll, Rhiannon is urged to have a child – in this way a commitment to the world of mortals is pushed upon her. However, the baby is stolen away, and Rhiannon's serving women, fearing punishment, smear her hands with the blood of a puppy, as she sleeps, exhausted after the birth. Rhiannon wakes and asks for her son, whereupon the women tell her that she killed and ate him in a fit of madness, and that they were powerless, in the face of her supernatural strength, to prevent this.

Rhiannon, in her wisdom, knows quite well that this is a fabrication, but she faces the penance that has been decreed for her, namely that for seven years she must stand at the city gate and offer to carry all who come to the court, upon her back. So the goddess becomes a beast of burden. At any time she might choose to return to the Otherworld, but she stays, hoping that her lost son will at some point be returned to her and she will be exonerated.

In another part of the kingdom a man called Teyrnon is regularly losing his colts to an unknown predator, so he decides to lie in wait for the creature. When a huge claw appears through the barn door he lops it off and pursues the shrieking creature into the night, to no avail. When he returns he finds a new-born babe beside his mare,

along with the colt. Teyrnon and his wife raise the child as their own, but soon the boy's likeness to Pwyll is unmistakable. Teyron takes the child back to his rightful parents. Rhiannon is freed from the burden of guilt, and from her onerous duty and takes her place again as queen and goddess.

Rhiannon is the White Mare of the Sea, and she is Queen of Elphame, who rides with the faery folk from the hollow hills – so she is a traveller between worlds, a bringer of the divine and magical. Somewhere in the heart of Sagittarius there is a desire to bring the fire of the gods into mortal hearths and to experience something expansive, something extraordinary, even if only for a moment – many Sagittarians are 'walkers between the worlds' in some sense. Rhiannon shows there is a price to pay for this, and it is the price of humility, the price of accepting burdens, of doing the work of a beast, perhaps, in order that inspiration may take shape. Here is a message for Sagittarius – it is that a little humility goes a long way and may eventually pave the path to greater enlightenment. It also conveys that while Sagittarius can never be totally confined or expected to knuckle under for a long, acceptance of material burdens at some point is the only way to bring the inspired into the here and now. Rhiannon is another personification of the Sagittarian 'wound' that we encountered with Chiron.

■ PRACTICE AND CHANGE ■

- If you are a Sagittarius, then in some sense you are an adventurer, and part of being yourself is to take chances and gamble a little with life.
- Even though you may have been taught not to recognise it, there is a part of you that reaches out for a real expansion of consciousness, and can see beyond the everyday. Think about what this might mean to you and bear it in mind.
- Perhaps people think you are 'clever' but your real gift is wisdom. Wisdom is deeper, wider and often quiet. Ask yourself what wisdom means to you.
- Never let concentration on the bright side mean you do not face real pain and problems. Cultivate the true optimism of faith in yourself rather than the false one of denial.
- Do not be afraid to fail. Acceptance of real limitations can set you free – free from time wasting and self-deception. Recognising what you can't do frees you to do what you can do. Life is the art of the possible.
- Give yourself permission to be 'different' if that is how you feel. One Sagittarian I know was conscious of an uneasy sense of being different, but when she found imaginative friends who appreciated her gift for poetry she felt much more at home.
- Most Sagittarians need an injection of a little humility at some point. This is not to clip wings, but to introduce some moderation that makes relationships more viable and achievement more real. This may open your eyes to reality and from there to the achievement of something really exciting. Sometimes you have to fall from the high horse to find yourself gazing up at the stars.

2 Relationships

Love, free as air, at sight of human ties,
Spreads his light wings, and in a moment flies

Alexander Pope, *Eloisa to Abelard*

The tale of Sagittarius is usually one who loved not wisely but too widely. Sagittarius often whole-heartedly enjoys other people's pleasure and gains comfort from being part of the larger social group. Intimacy is not always easy for the Archer, and while you may dash into relationships with urgency and naïvete, often the fire has gone out and there's nothing for it but an awkward exit. Yes, Sagittarius loves love, and it is well known that 'all the world loves a lover'. Some of the most charming and glamorous characters have a strongly placed Sagittarius, and this wild card of the zodiac can often be the King or Queen of Hearts. Sagittarius can be a promiscuous sign, restless in bed as everywhere else. However, deep inside what most Sagittarians want is a relationship of transcendant meaning, where spirit, soul and senses are alike assaulted by an all-powerful emotion and where pathways are opened to the glorious! They don't want much! Needless to say, this sort of Holy Grail is not found under every bush, and Sagittarius may go from partner to partner, believing each time that paradise has been found, only to wake up one wet Monday to find they are trapped in the commonplace again. The partner may be blamed for being a 'drag' – which partners of Sagittarians often seem to become. Try exploring the possibilities inherent in this relationship. After all, it did look good once, and it could again, with a little sprinkle of stardust.

Sagittarius is sometimes hooked on freedom and you may destroy all in your path to get it, like an addict grabbing for the next 'fix'. Generally a trusting person, you can become almost paranoid about partners scheming to trap you. However, you can feel lonely, like anyone else. Perhaps it is more true to say that Sagittarius requires independence. Nothing makes you feel more important and interesting than having a possessive partner to jib at. Most partners cannot help sounding just a little petulant if they are left all dressed up and nowhere to go, because Sagittarius has wandered elsewhere, and in this way you avoid a great deal of potential emotional pain. After all there isn't much risk of rejection, if you're always first to the door. However, if you are given enough rope, in the end you will usually cheerfully tether yourself. This idealistic sign *can* be faithful and often wants to be. But you need to find your own way.

■ SAGITTARIAN SEXUALITY

With Sagittarius sex often has a 'now or never' quality, for if the moment has passed the flames may dampen and Sagittarius may decide not to bother. For all the rampant reputation, sex for the Archer has an elusive quality. If the fantasy element isn't quite right, if there is no danger or intrigue, the cold wind of boredom can blow away the last vestiges of passion. You may well promise more than you can deliver in bed, and some Sagittarians, despite countless amours, may say sincerely that sex is overrated. To others sex is a glorious festival, a riot of the spirit and the senses and something that has more than a hint of the celestial. Sex is a matter for the soul, rather that the body. For you it simply is not enough to copulate. If all that is happening is a meeting of the flesh you will probably not be able to concentrate, and desire just disappears. Partners of Sagittarians may feel a little desperate at this, for how can anybody be eternally exciting and different? Well, you can't, and it's up to the Sagittarius. Best to give you your head and let you carry your partner along. Sometimes it may be a bareback ride to somewhere wild; at others they will feel they have been thrown off into a puddle. They should shrug their shoulders, try not to mind and above all, shouldn't take it personally. You may not be the most considerate or consistent lover, but you are never boring. The only predictable thing is that the ardour will surely rekindle, sooner rather than later, if you are not pressurised.

Female Sagittarius

Sagittarian ladies may find themselves in something of a quandary, sexually, because while their nature demands independence and equality, at the same time they like assertive males who will in some sense 'take' them. Naturally many men are becoming very wary of such situations. Taking Ms Sagittarius's strong personality and self-sufficiency to be the signal for behaving like a 'new man' they may treat her with consideration, gentleness and even deference. They may have the door slammed in their face by an outraged Sagittarian, whose secret fears of 'not being a proper woman' (not unusual in any of the Fire signs) have been confirmed by this cool treatment. Like her male counterpart, this lady likes excitement and erotica. She likes to be able to put her mate on something of a pedestal, and it's a strange fact that once her respect has gone, so has her desire. Like all the mutable signs, there is often a duality in Ms Sagittarius. Yes, 'respect' is an important matter, not just for her but for her partner. She expects to be respected, but she is also powerfully aroused by situations where she is in danger of losing a great deal more than respect! For her, fantasy is very important, along with ardour and overwhelming desire. She likes to be taken by storm, not only by her partner but by her own feelings. In bed she is eager and very responsive – she's worth the effort!

Male Sagittarius

Mr Sagittarius often does his best to live up to his reputation as a stallion, but the truth of the matter can be that Mr Sagittarius has a few sexual problems, and these may range from periodic total disinterest to premature ejaculation and impotence. Occasionally, fear of commitment may give rise to the rarer problem of inability to ejaculate. Of course, this isn't universal, but when it happens it stems from the fact that, to Sagittarius, a body is a clumsy and most unsatisfactory vehicle to have to go around in. Failing a transition to pure spirit, Mr Sagittarius has no option but to adapt to its limitations, and he does this by trying to pretend they aren't there. Sagittarius can set himself impossible standards. Youth should be eternal and so should erections. Younger Sagittarians may be oversexed tearaways and older ones may try to escape from reality into sporting perpetual wall-to-wall tans and designer jeans overhung by a fifty-year-old paunch. Failure inevitably follows their overblown expectations, leading to the well-known cycle of anxiety, creating more failure, creating more anxiety. This may sometimes be offset by escapades that put Don Juan to shame, or tall tales of their studdery. Others recede into a philosophical attitude or take off for long walks over the hills, but these men are often only marginally more adapted. So is this man a hopeless lover, not worth bothering with unless one is prepared to bare all in the city-square fountain or wait for a trip in a hot air balloon? Not at all. It means again accepting that Mr Sagittarius needs the fantasy element and letting him provide it. It also requires the realisation, on the part of Sagittarius, that no physical limitation can ever cage the spirit. Some Sagittarians like to tell stories while they make love. The more fortunate can get high on the voltage of the encounter. If you can enter their world you can share in the fun.

The loves of Zeus

The exploits of Zeus/Jupiter, Graeco-Roman king of the gods, are well known in myth. As a lover he was insatiable, his adventures rendered all the more delicious because of the constant attempts of his wife, Hera, to frustrate him. As part of his seduction plan, Zeus would assume many different shapes. To Leda he appeared in the guise of a swan, resulting in the birth of the twins, Castor and Pollux; to Danae, mother of the hero Perseus he came as a shower of gold; to Alcmena, mother of Hercules, he assumed the shape of her husband, Amphitryon. Other notable shapes he took were that of a cloud and a bull.

Zeus had to hide his mistresses from the jealousy of Hera, but one of them, poor Semele, was discovered. Semele was aware that her 'husband' was king of the gods, and she was exceedingly proud of this fact. One day Hera went to her, disguised as an old woman, and on hearing about her husband she broke into a cackle 'Are you sure of that, dearie? Is he really Zeus himself?' she said. 'Does he appear to you in all the shining glory that surrounds him on Olympus?' Semele was tormented by doubt and when Zeus came to her she made him promise her one favour.

'Ask whatever you like, my love,' he assured her, 'it shall surely be yours.'

'Then appear to me as you do on Olympus, when you sit beside your immortal wife, Hera,' she implored.

Zeus was stricken, but as king of the gods he could not break his word. Rising to his feet and lifting his arms he became transfigured with glory. So fierce and bright was he that mortal Semele shrieked, fell back and shrivelled, instantly slain by his immortal brilliance. Zeus could not save her, but he saved their son, who was Dionysus and became the god of wine.

This is a story of Sagittarian extremes, from the many love affairs to the extravagant posturings of the Olympian ruler. It is also a tragedy, telling how one Sagittarian promise went too far, but even from this comes Dionysus, god of wine, bringing the good things of life so beloved by Sagittarius into the mortal realm. Zeus is a benevolent and generous partner to his many mistresses, despite being less than loyal to Hera. He is bound by his word, even though it means destroying what he holds dear, speaking of the idealism that many Sagittarians display. It is worth noting that Sagittarians and their partners may get well and truly 'burnt' by Sagittarian expectations, for although Sagittarius may appear unscathed this is often more apparent than real. Finally, the ability of Zeus to shape-shift hints at the plasticity of Sagittarius and your talent for transferring to another dimension. Perhaps the real meaning of love to Sagittarius is an opening of the doors of perception on to something wonderful, something divine. You aim high, and some arrows fall short, but no one can say you didn't try!

SAGITTARIUS WOMAN IN LOVE

Despite her tomboy exterior the Sagittarian lady's dreams are often all white lace and soft focus. She wants love to be wonderful and to be treated like a princess, and she may indeed be feminine and sexy enough to tempt any handsome prince. However, her tendency to launch herself at life and love in a series of power drives doesn't always do her any favours. Her exterior is sometimes 'jolly-hockey-sticks' or bluestocking, or a combination of both.

Before every female Sagittarius gets the impression that she has little sex-appeal, let me assure you that this is very definitely not the case! The get-up-and-go and flair of Ms Sagittarius is tantalising and magnetic to many men, and the lust for life of the Sagittarian female is sexy in the extreme. No one can look glamorous with quite the pizzazz of Ms Sagittarius, when she is at ease with herself. Take Tina Turner as an example. The Sagittarian rock singer appears to possess the gift of eternal youth, endless energy and inspired talent, perhaps drawing upon the spiritual well of her Buddhist beliefs.

Ms Sagittarius is capable of tremendous devotion. If she is in love she will throw all her considerable enthusiasm into the plans and dreams of her mate – and all caution to the winds. She is proud, fierce, passionate and loyal – but if she is disappointed she rarely hesitates to move on. Usually she is open about her feelings and her lover may bask in the truth or be blistered by it, depending on the circumstances. She is rarely coy or teasing, and if she says 'yes' she means it. She does not manipulate or prevaricate, what you see is what you get – but her lover should take a good, deep look. He shouldn't let her sincerity and apparent simplicity fool him into thinking she is easily won and kept. This woman wants to be overwhelmed with love, but that is not all she wants, and despite all her devotion there is part of her that can never be committed. She will never swap her walking boots for the cosy slippers of domestic bliss – she wants adventure and excitement. Whether this is mental or physical depends on her taste. Her lover should travel with her if he can, but if not leave the back door unlocked and be interested in her accounts of her experiences when she returns. If it's a smooth little canter he wants, better get off right now, but if it's a gallop to Shambhala and back again, before dawn, he should hold on tight and prepare for the ride of his life.

SAGITTARIUS MAN IN LOVE

Mr Sagittarius is living proof of the saying that 'A man chases a woman till she catches him'. This man loves the thrill of the chase but he sometimes falls into a relationship like an absent-minded hunter caught in his own bear-trap. Others charge into commitment like a commando on a raid, only to realise, too late, that escape has been cut off and that life is a horror story of mortgages and mother-in-law. Some Sagittarians have an earnest, burning desire for a meaningful relationship while others have an almost pathological fear of getting hitched. Whatever the case may be, Mr Sagittarius does not want the commonplace. He is on the track of some ideal, rather like a cross between Plato, and a schoolboy trying to catch sight of the Lesser Spotted Paradise Bird.

It is often said that women are drawn to 'dangerous men' and many male Sagittarians fit that category. Flirtatious and devil-may-care, casual, charming and untamed, Mr Sagittarius can have all the charisma and speed of a motor-racing driver. Every woman is secretly convinced that she can be the one finally to tie him down, and he does nothing to dispel that impression. Some Sagittarians have a throng of hopeful maidens before them and behind them – their old lovers they retain as friends, each one secretly hoping that he will come to his senses, in the end, and realise that she is 'the one'. This year, next year, sometime, never – Sagittarius is often the most carefree bachelor in the zodiac. However, such machismo is becoming outmoded, and far from being thrilled many women are quite aware that instead of being excitingly 'dangerous' the commitment-phobe is actually somewhat immature. Such men may be lopsided, having no connection to their own 'feminine' side. What is left for Mr Sagittarius?

Of course, a great deal is left and despite all the above there are Sagittarian men who make inspiring and committed partners. Such a man is warm, loving and always interesting. He pours his considerable idealism into making the relationship something special.

However much he loves you, Mr Sagittarius is never likely to run to sensitivity, or even tact. He'll give your waist a playful squeeze, but stop romance in its tracks by saying 'You've put on weight, gal'. All the same, at Christmas time he gives you a silk camisole in a size that hasn't fitted you since you were sixteen, so it's obvious that despite his clumsy tongue, to him you're still that sexy sylph he fell in love with. Enter his dreams with him and his love will burn brightest, but look elsewhere for emotional support because he probably just doesn't know what that is.

GAY SAGITTARIUS

Gay Sagittarians all things being equal, have an easier time than many, for they are usually open about their feelings and unabashed, and will enjoy the adventure of a homosexual encounter, or discover they are 'gay' with excitement and the impulse to explore. For male Sagittarian gays there may be a problem in that hunter hunting hunter, with all the enthusiasm of Sagittarius, can result in a formidable number of partners, with dangers of infection that are sadly all too well known. Occasionally Sagittarians of a more traditional bent will suffer guilt about their preferences and may tangle themselves uncomfortably in morals and philosophy. Sagittarius's rather slender connection to physical reality can go one of two ways here. Either there may be a feeling that physical desires should be subordinated to spirituality, and so anything that might offend the larger social milieu or traditional moral values should be suppressed. Others will appreciate that physical love is an avenue to the spiritual, and that love is love, and it is of the divine, whether shared with members of the opposite sex or one's own. Often Sagittarius will not even notice the preferences of another person, unless that person happens to interest him or her sexually. Straight Sagittarians may occasionally censure what they do not understand, on ethical grounds.

SAGITTARIUS LOVE TRAPS

The Don Juan syndrome

Don Juan is well known as the ultimate philanderer – and, of course, we can have Doña Juana, too. As we have seen, Sagittarius may indeed go from lover to lover. More lies behind this than mere inconsistency, boredom, impulsiveness, etc. Here there is a real fear of intimacy along with a burning desire for it. Driven by a need to get close, Don or Doña launches into sexual encounter, only to find that closeness evokes a restlessness and even fear. So the liaison is broken, but the need is not assuaged, and it impels the Sagittarius into another encounter, and another, and another . . . . Far from being a tale of glamour and enticement, this is a sad saga of loneliness. Don and Doña do not really feel lovable and must continually prove their desirability, but getting the whole world into their bed can't fill that emptiness inside.

Of course, Dons and Doñas are not exclusively Sagittarians, but a strong Sagittarius can make this reaction more likely. The only way out of it is to take a good look at oneself and to get some professional help, if necessary. What do you *really* want? And what are you afraid of? Lots of time and courage may be needed to find the answers, but the potential reward can be a fulfilling relationship, and time freed up in a bed-hopping life for more productive pursuits!

Serial monogamy

The modern trend towards serial monogamy could have been invented by Sagittarius! Despite all the Sagittarian need for freedom there is within them a traditionalist and moral streak that does tend to matrimony. Unlike Aquarius, that other freedom freak, Sagittarius is not necessarily committed to flaunting convention, and would usually rather find liberty within the system. Because of this Sagittarian ethics are a little 'creative' at times! These factors, combined with the natural impulsiveness, can sometimes mean marriages strung like beads through life, along with alimony payments, access arrangements and all the sordid paraphernalia that Sagittarius would far rather pretend did not exist.

Sagittarius has never been a lover of closed doors, but while the urge for freedom may be one problem, the urge to enter another relationship poses another. This is in contrast to 'Don Juan' – this Sagittarius is not as fearful of intimacy, but is warm, impulsive and addicted to saying 'yes'.

SAGITTARIUS AND MARRIAGE

Despite all we have said about Sagittarian unreliability, dislike for commitment, addition to freedom, etc. many Sagittarians are living proof of the phrase 'Marry in haste, repent at leisure'. Of course, Sagittarians rarely pretend that all is well when it isn't. Martyrs they are not, and they would prefer to walk off into the sunset with only the coat on their back, rather than stay and suffer for the sake of security. However, things are not always so simple, for Sagittarius may become very discontented and yet not leave, simply because of the sneaking feeling, born perhaps from experience, that the grass on the other side of the hill is *not* greener and there may be more mileage in complaining that their partner doesn't understand them.

Certainly some of the most committed and happy single girls and bachelors come under the sign of the Archer, but often Sagittarian good humour, respect for principles and tendency to put all of themselves into whatever they undertake makes them warm and interesting partners.

■ WHEN LOVE WALKS OUT – HOW SAGITTARIUS COPES

Some Sagittarians don't notice when their lover has left, and may wonder absently why no one has done the washing up! It may take them years to wake up to the fact that the love of their life was lost through their carelessness – or maybe they simply never really cared. It is possible for Sagittarius to become deeply depressed, although this is not usually accompanied by a downcast air but rather by a brittleness that makes companions uneasy, without knowing why. Remember that if you choose to hide your feelings, the price of maintaining that bright and breezy image is that you suffer alone, and maybe for longer. More importantly, if you convince yourself you don't care you are lying to yourself, and while you may be keeping the pain at bay, consciously, you are denying yourself healing.

Starting afresh

It is possible that wounded Archers may rush headlong into another relationship, and some spend half their lives 'on the rebound'. Well, don't! If that special person is worth it he or she isn't going to disappear overnight, and you won't burst if you don't declare your passion immediately.

Some often bitten Sagittarians do become embittered, strange as this may sound, and clothe this in philosophies about the sad way of the world, or the opposite sex, until they disappear inside themselves. They can do with being jostled out of this by some plain speaking and robust humour.

■ PRACTICE AND CHANGE ■

- Do you want a 'steady' relationship? And are you having trouble achieving this? Remember that it is fiction that there is just one special someone waiting out there for each of us. Relationships are about the right time, the right place and about what you put into them. You have a great deal to offer a relationship – you just have to decide to do it.
- No relationship can be transcendent all of the time, and to expect this is to set yourself up for disappointment. Think of your partner as a companion on a glorious quest, rather than the object of the quest, and adventure together.
- Any relationship is going to require some commitment. You may like to think about what this means to you, and how much you can or can't 'commit'.
- Sexual 'problems' if they arise, are definitely not due to the fact that you are in any way inadequate or not a 'proper' man or woman. Stop trying to prove things to yourself and treat yourself with gentleness. Turn finding the cause of your problems into an interesting quest.
- Remember that nothing can cage your spirit.
- You need to develop a little tact. Try saying less and thinking more around the one you love. There really is no point in causing hurt. And remember a simple 'I'm sorry' goes a long way, and much further than 'You're so *sensitive*!'
- Many mottos seem to have been coined especially for Sagittarius. 'Look before you leap' is the best.
- If you choose to hide your feelings you are choosing to deprive yourself of help. Get yourself all the help you can so you can get out of the doldrums quicker. The rest of us need your happy-go-lucky grin!

3 All in the family

One would be in less danger
From the wiles of the stranger
If one's own kin and kith
Were more fun to be with

Ogden Nash, 'Family Court'

A Sagittarius in the family can make life exciting all around – except for that time they go absent without leave and everyone is looking for them. This is bad enough when they're twenty-five, but at the age of five it can be alarming indeed! It may be late on Christmas Eve before you know whether to count that Saggie relative in for a slice of the turkey. Sagittarians often enliven family life by their sheer enthusiasm and inventiveness, or deepen it by their thoughtfulness.

SAGITTARIUS MOTHER

This lady finds motherhood one of the most exciting of life's adventures and she will weave endless dreams around the cradle of this new scrap of humanity. Despite her happy-go-lucky nature, Sagittarius mother takes her role very seriously, vividly appreciating that this child is a precious bit of the future, entrusted to her care. She may think for a long time before committing herself to motherhood, however, nonetheless somehow finding herself pregnant by accident. Of course, she absolutely *hates* to be tied, and will possibly be fearful of this and also of not being a good enough mother, simply because of her itchy feet. Baby may well be carted around the neighbourhood in a baby-sling or spend half of its life in a car-seat, so the children of Sagittarian parents are often alert and adaptable. It is best for Sagittarius to have regular help in the house, for she will be a much better and more relaxed mother if she is not chained.

Most days Sagittarius mum will cope efficiently and speedily with bathtime routines, housework, etc. Of course, she doesn't like dusting and vacuuming, but she will tend to get this over with as quickly as possible – she's adept at short cuts and may have her house looking like a scene from *Homes and Gardens,* as long as you don't open any of her cupboards! Although her children will have the basics she doesn't bother with details, and sometimes little Johnny may emerge with odd socks on, because it looked such a lovely day she couldn't wait to get out into the country, or to see friends. And if you look closely, Mum's wearing odd socks, under her jeans! Sagittarius mother is rarely a disciplinarian, but she can be impatient and lose her temper in dramatic, but short-lived style. While she's mad, however, her verbal arrows can strike home, and Sagittarius mum may need to remind herself that a child will remember forever such phrases as 'I'm disappointed in you' yelled in desperation because for the third time in a month the school jumper has been lost (junior takes after mum!). It is true that Sagittarius mother does expect high standards, but she's resourceful with help and advice.

Sagittarius mother's cooking ranges from the exotic to the thrown-together. One evening it may be a four-course Indian banquet, served for twenty friends, the next night it's couscous and nut paté, and the next burritos and salsa. Just when the family think she's chef of the year she rolls in late and dishes up beans on soggy toast. She's never boring!

As her children grow she tends to become closer to them – she's not at her best at the nappy stage. They can become mates and travelling companions, and she will love to chat in the kitchen with teenage friends, especially if they are on foreign exchange. She can become very excited about her children's studies and may enter into them enthusiastically. Children should always be honest with Sagittarius mum and express feelings openly and directly. She hates falsehood and is either immune to manipulation or such a pushover they feel guilty. If they make her their dear friend, they will be paying her the compliment of her life!

SAGITTARIUS FATHER

This dad can be hard to find for one reason or another. Either he's buried behind a pile of dusty books or off on the golf course, or to a football match, or . . . just somewhere. 'Look Mummy – is it a bird, is it a plane?' 'No, dear, it's Daddy, hang-gliding over the Eight-till-Late'. Some Sagittarius dads are just absent minded, and lets face it there are many Sagittarians who bury themselves in the telly-and newspaper routine, too. Others have escape down to a fine art, and I knew one Sagittarian *paterfamilias* who achieved his dream – a mobile home all of his own – by the simple expedient of a divorce that existed mostly on paper, giving him sexual freedom and unlimited access to his family home and tribe of children, whenever he chose to wander there – with his washing!

Having said this, many Sagittarians make exemplary fathers, combining a sense of duty and tradition, with a sense of fun. Sagittarius father is often bemused by the baby stage, it is true, and may wonder what on earth he has done. But as soon as the child starts to move and to show an interest in life, then he becomes gradually more and more fascinated. He can be a real pal and at his wonderful, energetic best when it comes to outings and holidays. If he is a sporty Sagittarius the boys and girls can tag along, blissful and filthy. If he is of the more intellectual bent they will be mesmerised at his remarks about time-warps and pyramidology – and wait until he actually *takes* them to the Valley of the Kings! He will if he can!

Some Sagittarius dads can be a bit lazy, and too laid back to take the children into their world, but the children are usually free to find their own way to the woodshed. This man isn't usually a disciplinarian although, like his female counterpart, he may have high standards. He may be over-honest, especially with the girls, and he may need to remind himself that it is a father's job to affirm the femininity of his daughter, without, of course, crossing boundaries. He may slap her on the back or make jokes about her freckles, but never say what's on his mind – namely that's she's the prettiest little thing he ever saw – because it sounds too soppy. This father can be a real mate and a fund of wisdom. He should not be afraid of letting his children get close.

THE SAGITTARIUS CHILD

This little one is likely to need lots of contact and stimulation. He or she will benefit greatly from being carried around in a sling or backpack, and is far more likely to settle if there is human noise around – at the tiny stage that is! Later on 'settling' is not going to be the favoured activity. Little Sagittarius doesn't want to miss anything and will still be awake at twelve if there's a party on. As the schooldays unfold the young Sagittarius is often living proof of what psychologists have discovered – namely that children study and absorb much better when they have the radio or hi-fi on.

Little Sagittarius can be clumsy. Life is just too exciting to be worrying what your hands and feet are doing all the time. Keep the medicine cupboard well stocked – and well locked! Paediatric wards are full of bleary mums with bouncing little Sagittarians who have been kept in 'for observation'. Sagittarius girls are often tomboys –

please don't *ever* say 'Behave like a lady'. Young Ms Sagittarius will have philosophy to back up her torn jeans – but inside she will be hurting and may carry this scar to her femininity for a long time.

Sagittarian children love to disappear into a world of fantasy through books, films and television, and they love to escape to the woods, barefoot, with a jam-jar. Yes, this is cause for worry today, and all the more so because these children wear their heart on their tee-shirt and will chatter to anyone they meet. However, preventing a Sagittarian from exploration is not a good idea, and is more likely to result in clandestine escapes through an open window! The best thing to do is to ensure that the younger Sagittarius has suitable company on escapades – and that parents make the time to take their child on as many excursions as possible.

The reasons why solo trips aren't a good idea need to be explained to young Sagittarius frankly, for your best hope of controlling them is to give them sound reasons, listen to and seriously counter all their resourceful arguments for why they should do what they want and if this applies to your little Sagittarius then stock up with books and videos to delight him or her. Better still, get Sagittarius their own PC and CD ROMs, so they can take off on 'Encarta'. Always, somewhere, somehow, there is an explorer trying to get out in Sagittarius, and this is at its most enterprising and excitable in youth. Treasure it.

Sagittarians can be gauche teenagers and may feel 'out of it' in the early teens. On the other hand, sense of adventure may rule the day and their sexual experiments may start young. I can't say there is any easy way for parents to cope with this, but again frankness helps.

Please do not make silly rules or any that are out of step with their companions. Sagittarius does have a sense of hierarchy and tradition – Sagittarian children will not break rules for the sake of it, but they will always seek independence and wish to preserve freedom. Sagittarius does not want to rebel, deep down – they want to respect their parents and to receive respect in return. If parents don't enter into their current enthusiasms and patronise or mock, they will soon have the tables turned!

Young Sagittarians may become extravagantly upset at times – they are generous with their misery, as with most other things, and the whole house may be in despair. Do not worry – this is unlikely to last more than a day, or a week at the most. There is just too much out there to interest and stimulate for Sagittarius to stay down for long. This youngster should be given sensible boundaries that bring them up against life as it is – an arena of endless possibilities, yes, but not of infinite resources. Pocket money, for instance, should not be elastic. If they blow it all by Monday night then they'll have to do without until the weekend. Always try to find the happy medium which guides but does not restrict. Don't ever dampen their enthusiasm – you can't anyway for long and you may set yourself up to be ignored.

If you can allow this young person as much freedom as possible, if you are prepared to meet them on their own level – which may be surprisingly high – and enter into their adventures, if you can put up with their frank remarks about the new furniture that has just cost your arm and leg, and if your nerves can survive eighteen or so hair-raising years, from the time they leap out of their cots (at nine months) through the time the fire service had to rescue them from the top of the old oak tree, to that supreme moment when they call you at 2 a.m. because their old banger has broken down in the middle of Exmoor, then you deserve Parent of the Year award, and you will probably get it, in a wise, young friend who wants to take you with them when they go round the world.

SAGITTARIUS AS SIBLINGS

A Sagittarius brother or sister may be a champion, a clown, or a maddening tease and cheat. The honest Archer has an opportunist streak that can, paradoxically, become downright underhand. It has to do with Sagittarian lack of boundaries, and it can mean that their siblings just *never* win when playing cards, or anything else with them. This is bad enough if they like to win themselves, and most of us do. It is even worse if Sagittarius has talked them into betting their last penny on the game, and then walks off with his or her squandered allowance augmented by their loss! However, the chances are that they will be generous at some time in the future – that is, if their siblings can get to them before their money has burnt a hole in their pocket.

Sagittarius may cheer brothers and sisters up when they're down, or laugh at them unkindly. This is never a sign to mince words and certainly not with a sibling. If Sagittarius thinks a sibling's new trainers are naff, they'll tell them, so they had better develop a thick skin. After all, it will help them to deal with all the tactless hulks life has yet to launch at them. If siblings can put up with this joker and see the best in them, they can make a good friend, for Sagittarius loves to be a friend, first and foremost. There is a place in Sagittarian hearts for family loyalty, as long as they do not feel chained by it. Sagittarius can show siblings the bright side, whatever has befallen. Just watch out for cling-film on the lavatory on 1 April!

SAGITTARIUS IN THE HOME

I have to say that Sagittarius and lack of space just do not go together, and I would urge you, if there is a lot of Sagittarius in your family, to do your utmost to get a big house! Many Sagittarians are extremely untidy and can turn a room into a heap just by walking through the door. Some have a habit of spreading themselves and their possessions over the entire house and into everyone's else's living space. They aren't invasive – just sprawling. Neither are they collectors – they just never get around to sorting out their broken tennis racquets, worn-out shoes, five-hundred copies of *National Geographic* and the stack of overdue library books quietly accruing fines the size of the National Debt.

If you really do have to cope with very little space, give Sagittarius as much of it as you can spare – perhaps that dusty cupboard under the stairs. Large cupboards in which to fling things are an asset – Sagittarius probably won't want to fuss around sorting out. I did once know a Sagittarius whose sense of moral purity was outraged by hairs in the drain, but he was a rarity. Mostly Sagittarians require heavy blinkers on the part of he or she who organises the household, for they simply do not notice mess, especially their own.

Give Sagittarius a room with a large window and plenty of light, if you can. Murals on the wall will help to create a sense of space and fantasy, and beds that fold into the wall or are built high with cupboards underneath are a good strategy. A shed or outhouse will help, if you have a sporty Sagittarius who owns sets of golf clubs and a racing bike. Cut down generally on ornaments and clutter of your own, for they just make the place look smaller.

Naturally, a Sagittarius who has been brought up in limited space, perhaps as part of a large family, will learn to keep his or her possessions well ordered, and it is no bad training for life to realise that one must adapt one's possessions to the available surroundings.

■ PRACTICE AND CHANGE ■

- Sagittarian parents, especially mothers, need to remind themselves not to feel guilty about needing space, stimulation and freedom, for nothing will drive you mad quicker than baby talk.
- Having said this, make sure you have sitters lined up. Families of Sagittarian parents will be doing a great favour if they make themselves readily available.
- Sagittarians need to take care that their fear of intimacy does not keep their children at arms length – and this may apply especially to dads. Of course, Sagittarians need intimacy, and it may be that very fact that bothers them. However, children grow up and away and there are only a few years of real closeness. In some ways, of course, they make more demands than a partner, but in others less. As a Sagittarius you value friendship, and that of your children will be a precious asset.
- Sagittarian parents may like to think seriously of getting paid help in the home, if they can possibly afford it.
- Sagittarian children need both freedom and sensible boundaries. It is a question of getting the balance right. Treat them with respect and be prepared to learn also from them – often that tousled head is a very old and wise one, on young shoulders.
- There is no harm in telling Sagittarians straight when they are infringing the liberties of others or saying hurtful things. Sagittarius can learn consideration like anyone else.
- If there is any sign of the spiritual seeker in young Sagittarius, this should be encouraged.

4 Friendships and the single life

But of all plagues, good Heaven, thy wrath can send,
Save me, oh, save me, from the candid friend

George Canning, *'New Morality'*

Friendships are naturally important to all of us, but those who are in relationships may have less time than single people to spend with friends. Because Sagittarius is often so keen to keep his or her freedom, it may well be the case that it is the partner who gets short shrift. However, some Sagittarians, never people to do things by halves, may become deeply absorbed in a new romance so that their old contacts think they have disappeared.

SAGITTARIUS AS A FRIEND

There are a few Sagittarians who tend to be abstracted, and some also who assume a Jove-like superiority to the rabble. There may be a judgmental streak in these. Most Sagittarians, however, are extremely gregarious, warm and outgoing. Your bright and breezy manners are in inspiration to others, and don't you love it! You are in your element holding court in an admiring crowd – or perhaps it would be more correct to say you like to teach and preach, just a little. No, I understate. You totally, absolutely, ecstatically adore playing the latter-day Socrates. This can range from the football fan who pontificates about Saturday's match to the truly learned Sagittarius who leads the meditation circle. In the words of Samuel Butler: 'Life is the art of drawing sufficient conclusions from insufficient premises'. Sagittarius is expert at drawing 'sufficient conclusions' and can explain and expound upon why the fact that someone threw away a drinks can will bring about the end of civilisation as we know it. This can get to the point where it is hilariously funny, and Sagittarius will usually see the joke.

Sagittarians are loyal friends, or indeed you intend to be. However, you are so addicted to saying 'yes' that you often promise more than you can deliver, and then disappoint. Many Sagittarians are inveterate name-droppers and will often range restlessly here and there, looking for 'where it's at'. This desire to be trendy has its roots in the Sagittarian need to find something meaningful, and this makes you feel you are eternally missing something.

Some Sagittarians are seduced by substitutes all their lives and never get past footloose and into philosophical. Such Sagittarians can make friends feel that they are forever missing something, out of time, past it – but they shouldn't buy that. They are feeling what you feel, for all your dash, flair and up-to-the-minute charisma. Inside you are insecure, and determined not to face the fact.

Of course, we know that Sagittarius is tactless. Friends shouldn't wail to you 'Oh, my nose is too big' because you will say 'Never mind, it goes with your face'. They shouldn't complain about the size of their ears, because you may suggest they find fame in a remake of *Dumbo*. Sagittarian women can often develop empathy, as they mature (and the men, too, sometimes!) and then friends get a really profound, human wisdom that can alter their perspectives and make them see that life – and they – are worthwhile. But they must know their Sagittarius well before they rely on this!

SAGITTARIUS AND THE SINGLE LIFE

Yours is one of the signs that is eternally 'single' in your heart of hearts, however committed you are to a relationship. Sagittarians who do not have partners usually adapt better than many. Some do retreat into 'splendid isolation' taking the attitude that the rest of the world isn't quite good enough – and thereby cover your feelings of rejection and loneliness.

However, you are not typically backward in seeking company. Yes, some Sagittarians are more introverted than others, but even quiet Sagittarians can find people to interact with who share their interests.

The principal pitfall for the Sagittarius who is single and doesn't want to be, is denial of need of intimacy. Such a person seems to be blown everywhere like an empty cardboard box, looking for something but never finding it unless he or she takes the trouble to explore exactly what is wanted. Then it may be found right under Sagittarius's nose.

The most important consideration for single Sagittarius is the opportunity to search *properly*. Some Sagittarians never respond to the urge for spirituality within them, but it is a potent force, and *every* Sagittarius really needs to find a belief or philosophy that has meaning for them, and to keep it perpetually under creative review.

You often like to spend your spare time finding out about foreign cultures or exploring arcane wisdom – you are not really interested in 'the facts' but where they may lead. A Sagittarius who has identified her or his spiritual quest is one of the happiest souls on the planet.

■ PRACTICE AND CHANGE ■

- Many Sagittarians prize themselves highly as friends (rarely ones for modesty!) and in this you have some justification. However, learn a little tact, for why should you wish to upset people? It certainly doesn't make you feel good. So, think before you speak.
- Develop the habit of saying 'I will if I can' rather than 'yes' whenever you are asked to do something mildly attractive. Remind yourself to get back to your friends and let them know your decision.
- If there is an element of the 'groupie' in you, ask yourself what it is that you are really seeking? What is so special about knowing the right people, being in the right places? Ask yourself what you are really looking for and look in your heart to find where you would truly like to be.
- If you catch yourself being superior, moralistic or judgemental, do pull yourself up and laugh at yourself. Others will probably laugh with you and your reward will be to know that you have cheered everyone up – again!
- If you have time on your hands, then you shouldn't need me to tell you to use it well, exploring some subject that fascinates you. There must be many. Don't waste your time dreaming or ranging here and there. Aim those arrows at a target.
- If you are single, rather than seeking out the trendiest hotspots, spend time on finding what is important to you.
- Are you a lonely Sagittarius? It's not like you to be such a sad soul. Put a smile on your face and go somewhere to mingle!

5

Career

My life was spent in one long effort to escape from the commonplace of existence

Sir Arthur Conan Doyle

The Sagittarian need for freedom is often quite literal. You hate four walls and closed doors. Usually you hate timetables even more. The more introverted of the sign still find it hard to cope with dreary routine that provides no mental stimulation. However, you can put up with a great deal if you feel it has a significant purpose

TRADITIONAL SAGITTARIUS CAREERS

The common denominator with all occupations suitable for Sagittarians is that most involve expanding boundaries in some form, or administering or searching for a 'higher' order – or that they merely offer freedom of movement. Sagittarius careers include:

- explorer
- traveller
- teacher
- scholar
- coach
- philosopher
- administrator
- lawyer
- the Church
- interpreter
- sporting pursuits
- work with animals
- travel agent
- publisher
- bookseller

WHAT TO LOOK FOR IN YOUR WORK

The majority of people work in large insurance corporations, sales offices, shops, banks and factories. Relatively few of us can choose a profession, train for it and find a fulfilling lifestyle, and as time progresses this is becoming more elusive.

To help you find a job that suits you, you need to bear in mind the spirit of what is recommended, not the specific occupation. One office job is not like another, one shop selling fashions may differ enormously from one down the street in terms of environment and opportunity. As a Sagittarius you need to make sure of several things when seeking employment:

- You will have a degree of freedom. This may mean literally being 'out and about', or it may mean freedom to fix your own schedule, or it may mean the mental freedom to explore and develop your ideas. Think about what sort of freedom you need and look for it in your work.
- Variety, too, is important to you. It will drive you mad to be doing the same thing, day after day.
- There should be a sense of exploration in your job. This may mean you simply find out something interesting each day by talking to people, or it may be more specific exploration, such as a research project.
- Somewhere, somehow your job should appeal to your ideals. This may not seem so important while you are young, for you may be more intent on buying a car and paying for a holiday. However, as you become older you will probably want to feel that what you do means something. This can be fairly mundane, on the face of it, such as feeling than your job in a supermarket has 'meaning' because you can help elderly ladies with their shopping. Or it may mean that you need a sense that your profession itself is deeply worthwhile and you may be

drawn to promoting charities or studying the law. If you are conscious of any emptiness in your career, think about this.

- On a day-to-day level you will need responsive companions, or you run the risk of being bored rigid. Seek colleagues who have a sense of humour or share your ideals.
- You should have the opportunity to move upwards or sideways in the organisation that employs you. You will not want to be doing the same thing for ever, however much it interests you at first.
- Many Sagittarians enjoy an element of risk. This may mean you like negotiating deals, dabbling on the stock market or staking all on some pet theory. Bear this in mind – it is better than the 'risk' element be conscious than to have it popping out at odd moments and playing havoc with your future.

So there is no need to feel that you have to look for a specifically Sagittarian job. Many Sagittarians would be aghast at mucking out stables, or might feel that the Church or the Law were extremely stuffy. Look for something that suits in its content and atmosphere, rather than its label. If it doesn't suit you then you will no doubt move on, but it will help to have an idea where you are going rather than be impelled by restlessness.

THE GURU

Sagittarians often like to feel they know a thing or two about some subject or other, and may not be slow to gather about them a following of believers. They may alleviate office boredom by holding forth on anything from reincarnation to their pet theories about the stock market. What they say may be 90 per cent valid, or 90 percent bullshit, but probably no one has the nerve to shout out that the naked Emperor has no new clothes – mainly because the Guru is so convincing, confident and superior.

Now, this person may be *en route* for the ashram, but colleagues have to get back to work. Guru may make them feel faintly petty and inferior for prioritising the mundane, but they shouldn't listen. This person *may* be wise, but if so he or she will be willing to talk to colleagues after work. On the other hand, the guru may be bored, lazy, or on an ego trip, or may have a struggle with the ordinary details of life and seek to escape from inadequacy in that department. The Guru may be afraid of being trapped, or afraid of failure. Colleagues should rest assured that no one who is half sensible will encourage them to mess up their job. If they need to get out, they should get out, but shouldn't hang around buying drinks for the Guru (funny how this person never seems to have any money) until someone flings them out.

There are plenty of wise people who are worth listening to, and many of them are, indeed, Sagittarians. However, there is a time and a place, as any wise person will tell you. Work in the day and go to your lecture, workshop or shamanic lodge in the evening, until you have decided on your path. Then by all means don robes and sandals and walk overland to India, if you wish, but be clear why you are doing it. And if you are a Sagittarius who has a calling to teach, make sure that you know what you are talking about and that it truly means something to you, not some moonlit escape route. Inspiration and beacons to follow are badly needed – you feel that – so make sure your 'beacon' burns with the flames of truth.

THE MAVERICK

This may be a super-salesman, or woman, with lots of charm and charisma – someone who always seems to be lucky and to be slapped on the back by the hand of fate. Or this may be a lone steer who grazes here and there, always heading for the green grass on the other side of the hill, but who never quite gets there. This person may be very successful, or may be avoiding involvement by a kind of superior detachment – the message is 'I know best, and until I can find a company that comes up to my exalted standards I'll make my own way.' Of course, independence is fine, and many Sagittarians genuinely prefer it. However, once more it may be fear of failure or rejection that keeps the Maverick apart. What if he or she were to be found wanting after commitment to a project? Better to hold aloof, and make one's own way.

The Maverick is often planning to set up on her or his own, and may suggest others join, too. They should think carefully about this. The Maverick may be a genius, or full of hot air. Those promises might not materialise. And will the Maverick take any of their wishes into account or give their ideas a try? If you are tempted by the Maverick you may have something of the Sagittarian gamester in you – will it be allowed a throw of the dice? And if you are a 'Maverick' why is it that you keep away from the herd? Is it from choice and the joy of it, or because you are afraid that the common old 'herd' might know a thing or two that has escaped you, like how to be contented and fulfilled? If you are to make the most of your independence, to make your schemes 'stick' and to find peace of mind, then you need to know yourself and understand your motives. Your potential is probably immense – don't waste it.

■ THE SAGITTARIUS BOSS

Those sensitive souls with the misfortune to have a Sagittarius boss, had better go to work wearing earplugs, blinkers and a suit of armour, or the slings and arrows of outrageous Sagittarius may have them sobbing in the toilet. The Sagittarius boss can be *embarrassing*. 'Surely you know the "e" in "sincerely" comes before the "l"' he or she may bawl across the office. The hapless employee keeps head down and blushes. 'No use hiding. They sell creams for red complexions – but none for bad spelling, more's the pity!' After a week of this sort of thing most people would feel like a wet rag by Friday. What it would be like if Sagittarius was there all the time, Heaven only knows. Luckily this boss is here and there and out of the office most of the time, so everyone has a respite.

Employees who can get used to occasional public humiliation may find there are bonuses to be had, also. For instance, Ms and Mr Sagittarius are equally loud and vocal with their praise. In addition, they are usually tolerant (unless someone offends that rather rigid moral code that some Sagittarians espouse) and the chances are they won't notice if employees are back late from lunch, because they don't get in until three themselves. Sagittarius is generally good humoured and understanding, as long as employees are honest, and probably this boss will be generous with money. Employees shouldn't inflict their pessimism on Sagittarius, and while they can indulge in a little light banter – in fact it will be positively to their advantage to do so – they should never challenge Sagittarius head on, on any matter he or she holds dear, for there is a part of Sagittarius that is always right, and it is at its 'rightest' in many Sagittarians in positions of authority.

This boss is unpredictable, but can out-think and out-work most people. Yes, Sagittarius may leave early for that special date, but will be in at seven-thirty next morning, to make up. If this boss likes an employee, he or she will not hesitate to bring this person on, and will acquire much satisfaction from any success. And, of course, not all Sagittarius bosses are loud and extravert – but most will not mince words if any mistakes have been made. Some Sagittarians are the quietly observant type, who miss nothing, especially the lucky break. Sagittarians are often very intuitive about business deals.

They may also be patron saints of lost causes – and some winners. Employees should make sure that they are in the latter category. They wouldn't be working for this boss if they didn't have potential, so they should brush up their stock of jokes. If all else fails, they can make their Sagittarius laugh (but respectfully, of course!).

THE SAGITTARIUS EMPLOYEE

It is important for employers not to fence this person in. If they believe that they will 'knock it out of him, or her' (whatever they conceive 'it' to be) then they should abandon the idea of employing Sagittarius and take a more commonplace soul. However, they will be missing out on a great deal, for this person can be a tonic to any company that gives him or her scope.

Sagittarius is rarely interested in 'the future' – and pensions, well, they're for the birds. The 'futurism' of Sagittarius is mostly sci-fi and millenarian prophesy, rarely is it to do with anything as stifling as 'prospects'. Sagittarius has faith in the future and lets tomorrow take care of itself. Sagittarius employees can throw light in cobwebby corners and may give employers some brilliant insights and plans. If they're gone for hours to get a signature, they will probably come back loaded with inspiration. If the job stimulates them, that is. If not, they may well have been at the bookies, or the bookshop.

Sagittarians are potentially wonderful employees. They are only 'unreliable' if the employer expects them to conform to practices which are – to them – just meaningless. If they are allowed to do their job creatively, they will draw up their own schedules and inject enterprise and imagination into what they do. Their enthusiasm should never be stifled or their schemes labelled 'wild', for although they may need pruning there is likely to be something very fruitful in all the ramblings. These people are often ahead of their time. Even quiet Sagittarians can throw some verbal gems into the puddle of complacency. A valued Sagittarius can endow wisdom and humour to any environment – and yes, that can add up to increased profits, too. This employee could well end up being a stake in the future.

WHEN UNEMPLOYMENT STRIKES

Most Sagittarians will shrug their shoulders at the prospect of unemployment, and some, it is true, will retain their optimism undented. Recalling all their many talents and believing in endless possibilities, they will go about searching for another niche and will find a better one. In these the Jupiterian positive attitude pays off: 'As you think, so you become', 'You make your own luck' – these people embody the truth of such sayings. For others, however, there is more bluster than lustre, and while they are vaunting their nonchalance inside they are very scared – and unwilling to show it.

Well, as we have seen in earlier chapters, there is no mileage in concealing your feelings – you who conceal so little. If you will find someone to talk to you are likely to recover your optimism sooner rather than later. And every Sagittarius *can* be positive. Remind yourself of what you are – *adventurous, optimistic, confident, expansive, lovable, lucky*. Repeat this three times before meals, when you get up and when you go to bed. It's your confidence pill.

Look for as many jobs or think about your future from as many different angles as you can – be resourceful, reject nothing. Think of this as an opportunity and turn the exploration into an adventure. Deal with the unpleasant (and, let's face it, scary) details *first*, such as your mortgage, if you have one, your insurances and benefit. If there are helpful souls who would help you to fill in forms, enlist their help and remember to make them feel good. Write to creditors and tell them what is happening. Then shoot a few arrows. Bet they lead you out of the wood into more sunshine than you've known!

SELF-EMPLOYMENT AND OTHER MATTERS

Sagittarians often take well to being self-employed. Inspired, independent, confident, intuitive and often self-motivating, self-employment suits them well. If you choose self-employment there can be several drawbacks.

The first is money, and, unlike your ideas *it is finite.* You must face financial restrictions and make plans. Second, try to be realistic. There is a fine balance between over-confidence and the conviction that you cannot fail, and the pessimism espoused by some folk. You are unlikely to be pessimistic, but make sure you get to grips with the real world.

Also, remember that your ideas may be brilliant but people may not be ready for them. Many Fire signs are ahead of their time. If this scheme isn't going to get off the ground through lack of faith on the part of others, then leave it be and do something else. Unless, of course, it matters to you idealistically. Then you will have to make up your mind just how much it is worth. Last but not least, you may have a tendency to dream – don't overdo it. Get off your butt and get going!

PRACTICE AND CHANGE

- In your work ensure you have variety, stimulation, as much freedom as possible and a sense of meaning. Don't sell your soul to the company.
- For various reasons you may stand aloof from the crowd, and indeed you may have insights not given to others. But be honest with yourself about what is going on. Nothing will ever be as good as your dreams, but it beats being eaten up by discontent.
- If you are a Sagittarian boss, remember that people often hear criticisms at 1,000 watts and compliments at a whisper. You want to get the best out of people, and sensitive souls are often resourceful. Also, not everyone can go at your pace, or have your enthusiasm. People may frustrate your ideals and ideas, but part of proving that positivity is working with this.
- If you are a Sagittarian employee, don't buck the system too much before you have given thought to what it means in terms of general values, and values to you. Some things that are tried and tested *do* work. And this job may have rewards for you – think about that before you are rude to your boss!
- If you are unemployed and/or going it alone enlist advice when and where you need it, and *listen.* There will be people who are able to do certain tasks better than you can by yourself or who can cheer you up. Don't get all hyped up with nowhere to go – dreams must have direction. Being 'grounded' doesn't mean being crushed, it means developing roots, which is the only way to grow.

6 Healthy, wealthy – and wise?

He is not a wise man who cannot play the fool on occasion

Sixteenth-century proverb

HEALTH

Astrological observations on health, even when based on the entire birth chart, may be of doubtful value or accuracy, because health depends on so many complex factors. What may we usefully say about the health of Sagittarius in general?

Many Sagittarians seem to exude health and energy. Health tends to come from within, and the positive Sagittarian attitude is a physical tonic. It is becoming accepted that when we are happy, amused and hopeful chemical messengers released into the bloodstream are conducive to good health. Sagittarius is no stranger to the dictum 'Laughter is the best medicine'.

However, Jupiter is the planet of excess, and Sagittarians have a lot of trouble being in any way moderate when it comes to indulging their passions. If these tend towards the studious the worst that may result is premature myopia. But many Sagittarians enjoy good food and good wine to a marked degree and do not know the meaning of 'elegant sufficiency'. This can be to the detriment of general health.

Being a Fire sign, Sagittarius is not well attuned to the physical, and so despite an immoderate love of the good things of life Sagittarius may forget to stock up on the basics. Sagittarian fridges may contain the odd mouldy yogurt and whiskered tomato, in addition to a bottle or two of fine Chablis and an excellent Camembert, bought in Normandy, of course – and just about ready to walk back there by itself! Trying to come to grips with bodily matters, Sagittarians may adopt diet fads and go overboard with macrobiotics, veganism etc., aware that they are searching for the absolute in health with no practical idea of how this might be achieved – if it were possible at all.

Sagittarius has a reputation for being very sporty, but I have known a greater proportion of Sagittarian who were frankly bored by a lot of sweaty grappling and 'silly' ball-chasing. However, those who do develop sporting interests – and this may be more likely with Sagittarius on the Ascendant – are often very good at it. They play to win, and while not being precisely 'bad' losers, will often deny they have lost when defeat is staring them in the face! Sagittarians may chase physical fitness as yet another Holy Grail, for it is hard for them to get their bodies into perspective and to accept their limitations. Sagittarian who have not developed their philosophical bent may do their utmost to stay the hand of time, and may become obsessive about fitness. Traditionally Sagittarius is said to be like horse-riding and archery – for obvious reasons! Many like a 'wheeled horse' too, and may go mountain-biking to where the air is free, in their spare time.

Hips and thighs

Sagittarius is said to 'rule' the hips and thighs, and because of this may be prone to injury or stress in this area, resulting in rheumatism or sciatica. In addition, the Sagittarian tendency to excess will naturally predispose towards heart disease and other disorders of the 'affluent' society, unless it is kept in check. Occasionally a strong Sagittarius may be one of the factors in obesity, the body 'expanding' instead of the mind.

Sagittarians should remind themselves that all things may be beneficial in moderation, most are destructive in excess, and that includes health fads, as well. Escapist Sagittarians may be tempted to drink alcohol to excess or use recreational drugs, because these open the doors of perception. They may do well to remind themselves that there are safer ways to expand their minds and these can be explored in the many groups and seminars offered today.

MONEY

Often a Sagittarian's best friend is the 'flexible' one, but nothing stretches to infinity. With the possible exception of Leo, no sign can vie with Sagittarius for sheer extravagance. However, the Leonine horror of humiliation can pose some restraint. Sagittarius knows no such boundaries! Blessed with endless faith in your ability to talk yourself out of anything, even a visit from the bailiffs, you spend money like it's going out of fashion. Despite the fact that you may have to go in disguise to your bank and are continually sought by the tax office, you never lose that indestructible belief that the universe shall provide. Maddeningly for the more provident, if often does! You often cannot resist a bet, and have the uncanny knack of picking a winner. Even if you don't, you shrug off the failure with a 'better luck next time'. Financially, you can be incorrigible and make life a running nightmare for your dependents.

However, I must say that while extravagance is a trait often found in this sign, the meanest person I ever knew was a Sagittarian! As usual, it is possible to trace the source of the dynamic, and in this case it resulted from a horror of becoming dependent and of facing failure and inadequacy. This is what can happen when that boundless faith gets eroded. Maybe the Sagittarian extravagance is harder on the nerves, but it has a heart-warming essence and that huge faith often rubs off.

Of course, there is no mileage in asserting that Sagittarius is like this, and that is that, because there is no doubt that improvidence can result in disaster and despair. The Bowery bum and the barefoot gypsy are Sagittarian archetypes, too, and these may have thrust themselves into penury, then adopting the life of a vagrant to convince themselves they don't care. Often heartache, broken marriages and homeless children train in their comet's tail. What is to be done? Well, there are several courses. First, the advice has to be to discover some of that innate wisdom and apply it to finances. They are *not* infinite. Second, some Sagittarians may need to ask themselves if they are not courting destruction in order to free themselves from material constraints to find some spiritual or artistic path. If this is the case, it is much better to arrive at this point consciously, while there is still some money in the bank. Although Sagittarius may be irresponsible, you can also be most responsible when it comes to those dependent on you, and you have a strong sense of the value of tradition. This is something that can be developed.

WISDOM

Sometimes it seems this sign has the premium on wisdom, and certainly we have spoken repeatedly about it in this book. Sagittarius's wisdom is something to cherish and it can save this sign from all its possible faults and excesses. Yours is the sign of the Seeker and the Teacher and it is vital for every Sagittarius to appreciate the important of spiritual quest in your life. You must also retain a sense of humour and avoid pomposity – friends are a great asset here if they are prepared to prick the bubble when necessary, as well as to cheer-lead. You are truly excited by new ideas and perspectives, and here the fiery arrows can ignite a beacon. You may need to recognise your abilities in this respect, without becoming inflated and patronising.

■ PRACTICE AND CHANGE ■

Health

- Develop moderation to offset your tendency to excess. This does not mean that you stop enjoying life – it means that you enjoy it more.
- Resist any temptation to 'escape' by using drink or drugs, for no real inspiration is found this way, and you run the real risk of being chained to a damaged body as a result.
- Whatever health regime you adopt, remember that you may expect too much of yourself. Be content with improvement rather than excellence.

Wealth

- If you are excessively extravagant, ask yourself if this is simply lack of restraint or a self-destruct mission designed to impel you into some sort of awakening. What are you trying to 'buy' – is it your happiness? Are you achieving it? – for that is most doubtful.
- The strategy of letting a partner manage some – or all – of the funds, can work, although it can be difficult. You will need to develop just a little humility and a lot of co-operation. On the other hand, it might be a relief to have budgeting responsiblity removed.
- If you are really wise you will recognise the 'wisdom' of restraint, as being a liberating factor.

7 Style and leisure

I have tried too in my time to be a philosopher; but, I don't know how, cheerfulness was always breaking in

Oliver Edwards, *Boswell's Johnson*

YOUR LEISURE

Many Sagittarians like to enjoy themselves in a big way. Unable to have a simple supper, they may have a five-course banquet. Failing that, they may grab a packet of crisps as they go out of the door and wash them down later with several glasses of something strong and fragrant. The middle way often eludes them. Sagittarians love to laugh. Many will clown around or play practical jokes. For others, leisure is something to be taken earnestly, and into which to throw all of your enthusiastic self. Sagittarians may plan social events on a large scale, or they may rely on the impulse of the moment. For many, spare time is devoted to the pursuit of study and exploration of other worlds, other concepts.

Sagittarius can turn a simple glass of wine into a glittering festival, or can be careless and 'absent'. Your energy and creativity is equalled only by your carelessness and abstractedness, when the matter in hand does not capture your interest. Some Sagittarians are 'culture vultures' or seekers-out of the trendiest spots, where they can hang out (hopefully) with a celebrity. These have an eternally restless air, and a fear that they are missing something. In this way Sagittarius can lead a glamorous life, without ever really enjoying it, because they have not stopped to ask themselves what they are truly seeking. This can look like fun, from the outside, and many Sagittarians are the envy of their acquaintances by the fact they seem to have 'bin there, done that, got the T-shirt' long before slower folk have even thought about it. For younger, extravert Sagittarians it may indeed be important and entertaining to get about as much as possible. If this is important to you, get out and do it, but if it palls be prepared to look elsewhere.

Sagittarius has a reputation for being 'sporty' that is often quite unjustified. However, Sagittarians who do enjoy sport are often supremely energetic and competitive. You like to win, and also to push back the boundaries of experience. You love to break records, including your own, pushing back human limitations. Sports favoured may be horse-riding, archery, javelin throwing, running, competitive swimming, or team games, in which Sagittarius will be heard shouting 'Pass it here'. Walking appeals to many people, and for Sagittarius the physical freedom of swinging arms and breathing deep of the fresh air can be a tonic. You may set out on ambitious treks, rucksack on back – you are less likely to favour an amble around the lanes on Sunday afternoon.

However, many more introverted or sendentary Sagittarians thoroughly relish the opportunity afforded by leisure to do some serious armchair travelling, finding out about other cultures, other modes of thought, or developing their knowledge of comparative religion and mysticism. Sagittarian leisure time is often devoted to spirituality, exploring world religions or holistic studies.

So, if you are a Sagittarius wondering how you might spend that time on your hands – and if sport does not appeal – consider shamanic groups, meditation, astrology, evening classes on geography, history, foreign cultures and languages, Egyptology, charitable work, past-life regression (although this should not be approached simply as a diversion) spiritual healing, work for your local church, chapel or spiritualist church, UFOlogy or even political campaigning. Balance mental activity with physical activity and remember that if you feel tired it may be because you are bored. If you see no suggestion here that interests you, think about pushing back boundaries, any boundaries, about exploring, believing, travelling, communicating – and expand yourself. What an exciting life this is!

Holidays

Sagittarians usually love travel, and while I have known Sagittarians who couldn't be bothered with the business of packing (and even one who was afraid to go abroad), that sensation of movement, of going somewhere – anywhere – is irresistible to many Sagittarians. The open road calls and you have something of the gypsy flowing in your veins. Also 'snob value' is not lost on many Sagittarians and you like to be able to mention – casually, of course – that you have been somewhere fabulous. The first lunar resort may well be packed with Sagittarians!

However, while you will rarely refuse the opportunity for travel, there is little point in depositing you on some sunny beach and expecting a fortnight's contentment! Some Sagittarians will welcome the opportunity to catch up on a little reading, but when this palls they will want to forage and explore. Sagittarian holidays should include variety and adventure and a chance to sample foreign culture where it's really at – enjoying goats' cheese and Greek wine in Arcadia, savouring the exotica of Bangkok or exploring the wild and remote in a Land Rover. Sagittarius likes to get the feel of a place, and will love to rub shoulders with the locals, learn some of the language and actually experience what it is *really like* to live and be part of this far-off country. Alternatively, some Sagittarians like to spend their holidays on a spiritual retreat, and some like a riot of night-life and dissipation – but nothing banal. And no package tours or coach trips, cooped up with blue-rinses and spectacles, all contact with the surroundings filtered through a sheet of thick glass, for such do not offer intensity or originality of experience.

YOUR STYLE

Sagittarian style is at once free and somewhat opulent. Many Sagittarians do not like to be restricted by their clothes – and many are careless of apparel, with frayed threads, flapping belts and ill-concealed safety-pins making them look like refugees from the Oxfam shop. Others like to dress in rich colours and fabrics, and some Sagittarians can be sharp and very trendy dressers. However, there is often still a touch of the casual, expressed in open collar or undone jacket. Sagittarius may buy expensive clothes, and wear them carelessly. You often buy on impulse, and you may not be bothered with the boring details of shopping, and will spend extravagantly and impatiently, with the excuse that your purchase has been chosen to last.

The faded glory of the Raj seems to hang around some Sagittarian homes. Chinese and Persian rugs – sometimes a little the worse for wear – rub shoulders with ebony figurines from Kenya, Russian samovars and Tibetan buddhas. Here there may be a mixture of ancient and modern, for Sagittarius loves tradition and exotica but will also want the very latest in technology, where appropriate. Thus Sagittarian cooks may use the best food-processors and electric mixers because they are too impatient to do things by hand. However, the microwave may be shunned because that isn't 'proper cooking' and the Aga used instead. Or state-of-the-art computer technology may be found in the study of a Sagittarius who rides a push-bike everywhere and has never bothered to learn to drive. I certainly knew one Sagittarius who felt spiritually free only in surroundings of spotless sterility, with the temperature maintained just above freezing point. Others will simply not notice mess, because they are preoccupied with something interesting. These are rarely souls who bother about details – the broad sweep is more their style.

So, if you are a Sagittarius choosing articles for yourself or your home, think flamboyant, exotic, labour-saving, speedy, casual, traditional, good quality, original, generous, cultural, foreign, imaginative, open, free, efficient.

Resist buying on impulse, and never buy where the shop will not accept returns. Take an interesting friend with you, if you find shopping boring, and turn the excursion into an adventure, or a laugh.

■ PRACTICE AND CHANGE ■

- You dislike the mundane, so don't be too impatient or lazy to turn an ordinary occasion into a celebration.
- When seeking leisure pursuits always think in terms of pushing back boundaries, educating yourself and expanding everything except your waistline.
- A reminder – if you are tired, you may be bored. Seek something interesting.
- Some form of 'spirituality' may be part of your recreational pursuits. If this is lacking, give it serious thought.
- Holidays should be as adventurous and varied as possible. Think about how you will spend your days on holiday – don't sign up in a hurry.
- Your style needs to incorporate as many aspects of you as possible. Try to combine a sense of freedom with quality, tradition and a flavour of the mysterious or foreign.

Appendix 1

SAGITTARIUS COMBINED WITH MOON SIGN

Our 'birth sign' or 'star sign' refers to sign of the zodiac occupied by the Sun when we were born. This is also called our 'Sun sign' and this book is concerned with Sagittarius as a Sun sign. However, as we saw in the Introduction, a horoscope means more than the position of the Sun alone. All the other planets have to be taken into consideration by an astrologer. Of great importance is the position of the Moon.

The Moon completes a tour of the zodiac in about twenty-eight days, changing sign every two days or so. The Moon relates to our instincts, responses, reactions, habits, comfort zone and 'where we live' emotionally – and sometimes physically. It is very important in respect of our intuitional abilities and our capacity to feel part of our environment, but because what the Moon rules is usually non-verbal and non-rational; it has been neglected. This has meant that our lives have become lop-sided. Learning to be friends with our instincts can lead to greater well-being and wholeness.

Consult the table on page 80 to find which sign the Moon was in, at the time of your birth. This, combined with your Sun sign is a valuable clue to deeper understanding.

Find your Moon number

Look up your month and day of birth. Then read across to find your personal Moon number. Now go to Chart 2, below.

January		February		March		April		May		June	
1,2	*1*	1,2	*3*	1,2	*3*	1,2	*5*	1,2	*6*	1,2	*8*
3,4	*2*	3,4	*4*	3,4	*4*	3,4	*6*	3,4	*7*	3,4	*9*
5,6	*3*	5,6	*5*	5,6	*5*	5,6	*7*	5,6	*8*	5,6,7	*10*
7,8	*4*	7,8	*6*	7,8	*6*	7,8	*8*	7,8	*9*	8,9	*11*
9,10	*5*	9,10,11	*7*	9,10	*7*	9,10,11	*9*	9,10	*10*	10,11,12	*12*
11,12	*6*	12,13	*8*	11,12	*8*	12,13	*10*	11,12,13	*11*	13,14	*1*
13,14	*7*	14,15	*9*	13,14	*9*	14,15,16	*11*	14,15,16	*12*	15,16,17	*2*
15,16,17	*8*	16,17,18	*10*	15,16,17	*10*	17,18	*12*	17,18	*1*	18,19	*3*
18,19	*9*	19,20	*11*	18,19	*11*	19,20,21	*1*	19,20	*2*	20,21	*4*
20,21	*10*	21,22,23	*12*	20,21,22	*12*	22,23	*2*	21,22,23	*3*	22,23	*5*
22,23,24	*11*	24,25	*1*	23,24,25	*1*	24,25	*3*	24,25	*4*	24,25	*6*
25,26	*12*	26,27,28	*2*	26,27	*2*	26,27,28	*4*	26,27	*5*	26,27	*7*
27,28,29	*1*	29	*3*	28,29	*3*	29,30	*5*	28,29	*6*	28,29,30	*8*
30,31	*2*			30,31	*4*			30,31	*7*		

July		August		September		October		November		December	
1,2	*9*	1	*10*	1,2	*12*	1,2	*1*	1,2,3	*3*	1,2	*4*
3,4	*10*	2,3	*11*	3,4	*1*	3,4	*2*	4,5	*4*	3,4	*5*
5,6,7	*11*	4,5,6	*12*	5,6,7	*2*	5,6	*3*	6,7	*5*	5,6	*6*
8,9	*12*	7,8	*1*	8,9	*3*	7,8,9	*4*	8,9	*6*	7,8,9	*7*
10,11,12	*1*	9,10	*2*	10,11	*4*	10,11	*5*	10,11	*7*	10,11	*8*
13,14	*2*	11,12,13	*3*	12,13	*5*	12,13	*6*	12,13	*8*	12,13	*9*
15,16	*3*	14,15	*4*	14,15	*6*	14,15	*7*	14,15	*9*	14,15	*10*
17,18	*4*	16,17	*5*	16,17	*7*	16,17	*8*	16,17,18	*10*	16,17	*11*
19,20	*5*	18,19	*6*	18,19	*8*	18,19	*9*	19,20	*11*	18,19,20	*12*
21,22,23	*6*	20,21	*7*	20,21,22	*9*	20,21	*10*	21,22,23	*12*	21,22	*1*
24,25	*7*	22,23	*8*	23,24	*10*	22,23,24	*11*	24,25	*1*	23,24,25	*2*
26,27	*8*	24,25	*9*	25,26,27	*11*	25,26	*12*	26,27,28	*2*	26,27	*3*
28,29	*9*	26,27,28	*10*	28,29	*12*	27,28,29	*1*	29,30	*3*	28,29	*4*
30,31	*10*	29,30	*11*	30	*1*	30,31	*2*			30,31	*5*
		31	*12*								

Find your Moon sign

Find your year of birth. Then read across to the column of your Moon number. Where they intersect shows your Moon sign.

Birth year	Moon number 1	2	3	4	5	6	7	8	9	10	11	12
1900 1919 1938 1957 1976	Cap	Aqu	Pis	Ari	Tau	Gem	Can	Leo	Vir	Lib	Sco	Sag
1901 1920 1939 1958 1977	Tau	Gem	Can	Leo	Vir	Lib	Sco	Sag	Cap	Aqu	Pis	Ari
1902 1921 1940 1959 1978	Lib	Sco	Sag	Cap	Aqu	Pis	Ari	Tau	Gem	Can	Leo	Vir
1903 1922 1941 1960 1979	Aqu	Pis	Ari	Tau	Gem	Can	Leo	Vir	Lib	Sco	Sag	Cap
1904 1923 1942 1961 1980	Gem	Can	Leo	Vir	Lib	Sco	Sag	Cap	Aqu	Pis	Ari	Tau
1905 1924 1943 1962 1981	Sco	Sag	Cap	Aqu	Pis	Ari	Tau	Gem	Can	Leo	Vir	Lib
1906 1925 1944 1963 1982	Pis	Ari	Tau	Gem	Can	Leo	Vir	Lib	Sco	Sag	Cap	Aqu
1907 1926 1945 1964 1983	Leo	Vir	Lib	Sco	Sag	Cap	Aqu	Pis	Ari	Tau	Gem	Can
1908 1927 1946 1965 1984	Sag	Cap	Aqu	Pis	Ari	Tau	Gem	Can	Leo	Vir	Lib	Sco
1909 1928 1947 1966 1985	Ari	Tau	Gem	Can	Leo	Vir	Lib	Sco	Sag	Cap	Aqu	Pis
1910 1929 1948 1967 1986	Vir	Lib	Sco	Sag	Cap	Aqu	Pis	Ari	Tau	Gem	Can	Leo
1911 1930 1949 1968 1987	Cap	Aqu	Pis	Ari	Tau	Gem	Can	Leo	Vir	Lib	Sco	Sag
1912 1931 1950 1969 1988	Gem	Can	Leo	Vir	Lib	Sco	Sag	Cap	Aqu	Pis	Ari	Tau
1913 1932 1951 1970 1989	Lib	Sco	Sag	Cap	Aqu	Pis	Ari	Tau	Gem	Can	Leo	Vir
1914 1933 1952 1971 1990	Pis	Ari	Tau	Gem	Can	Leo	Vir	Lib	Sco	Sag	Cap	Aqu
1915 1934 1953 1972 1991	Can	Leo	Vir	Lib	Sco	Sag	Cap	Aqu	Pis	Ari	Tau	Gem
1916 1935 1954 1973 1992	Sco	Sag	Cap	Aqu	Pis	Ari	Tau	Gem	Can	Leo	Vir	Lib
1917 1936 1955 1974 1993	Ari	Tau	Gem	Can	Leo	Vir	Lib	Sco	Sag	Cap	Aqu	Pis
1918 1937 1956 1975 1994	Leo	Vir	Lib	Sco	Sag	Cap	Aqu	Pis	Ari	Tau	Gem	Can

Ari Tau Gem Can Leo Vir Lib Sco Sag Cap Aqu Pis

Sagittarius Sun / Sagittarius Moon

You are the archetypal traveller, even if you never leave your arm-chair. Your mind is spanning the globe, exploring its exotic reaches and practices, and spinning off into space to experience the galaxy, also. Inner space also interests you and you may be a fund of obscure information on the workings of the human mind, philosophy and belief systems. You have enthusiasm for life and new ideas – which you know are not 'new' really. Be careful that you do not escape the pain that you need to experience for learning and growth, by distancing yourself through philosophy. Take care also that the belief system you adopt – and one is sure to be important to you, sooner or later – arises from your own appraisal of life rather than a moralistic tradition imposed upon you from without and adopted by you so you can feel wise or superior. You are potentially one of the wisest of souls – take the time to develop your powers of inward revelation.

Sagittarius Sun / Capricorn Moon

You can accomplish a great deal, although sometimes you may not believe it! Although you have plenty of enterprise and initiative, somehow it feels like driving with the brakes on, for you can see all the possible drawbacks of your brave schemes. You want to throw all caution to the winds and pursue your visions, which may be of a better world, a creative or moneymaking project or simply a good party, with friends, but instinctively you are urged to keep control of your emotions and your finances and not to sacrifice one iota of security. This can mean that you are continually falling flat over trip-wires of your own making, or it can mean that you are a highly practical achiever, and although rarely satisfied yourself, others admire your capabilities and results. By all means be careful, but also develop trust in life and, most of all, in yourself. You have the resources to cope.

Sagittarius Sun / Aquarius Moon

You are a great idealist and utopian dreamer, and to you all things seem possible at times. You may have an interest in sci-fi or the occult. Or you may be community orientated, involved in clubs and societies and adventurous schemes of all descriptions. Possibly you are none of these, more meditative, and yet I would bet that 'freedom' is one of your favourite words. It is probable that you are a 'busy' person, either in obvious ways, or internally, and you are likely to be able to accomplish much because you possess a measure of internal harmony. However, do remember to give freedom also to your emotions, and to those of others rather than seeking to escape them. Use your imagination to give space, to value and fully experience feelings, for these will enrich your perspective. There can be a great freedom, of the deepest sort, to be found in human intimacy. Try it – it may show you parts of yourself you'd not suspected.

Sagittarius Sun / Pisces Moon

Sometimes you really shock yourself. How could you have said this, done that, and been so utterly insensitive? Inwardly you recoil, but lo and behold it happens again! And then there are the times when you find you have withdrawn from something that looked fascinating, just because it didn't 'feel right', or given in to some silly sob story. Your inner conflict may cause you to feel resentful that you are missing out on something, at times. Conversely, you have the drive and vision to make your dreams a reality. Rather than losing sight of your own needs and own self in other people and then, at times, escaping from it all into a world of your own – or just being plain unreliable – concentrate on projects that both make you feel good and help others. It is okay to love yourself. Count to ten before you commit yourself and don't waste time on regrets.

Sagittarius Sun/Aries Moon

Well, you are a force to be reckoned with most of the time because you have the capacity to envision schemes and possibilities and the inner passion to carry them through. However, you prefer to sow rather than to reap – you may get things going but get bored with the practicalities and long-term commitment. Generally you expect to get your own way, and usually you do. Be careful you do not ride roughshod over anything and anybody, but seek rather to infect others with your enthusiasm. You are not a patient person, and sometimes, despite all your successes, you probably feel that you never quite experience what you wish for. Like sand it runs through your fingers, leaving you thirsting for a new venture. Stop searching for stimulation – what you need is inside you. Slow down, learn to meditate if you like, practise the simple activity of being where you are, seeing what is around you and experiencing yourself as a reality. You are alive, vital, important, even when you do nothing.

Sagittarius Sun/Taurus Moon

Your capacity for self-indulgence and sometimes indolence, combined with your love of escape in various forms, can result in achieving very little at times. At others, the wonderfully rooted pragmatism that you possess and your sensuous capacity combine with your broad-minded perspective to bestow an infinitely rich experience of life. You can be vividly creative, or a lounge-lizard with your head in the clouds – a contradictory picture, which actually fits you well! Truly your potential is enormous. You may alternate between bad habits and over-indulgence, and escapism and denial. Do not do this. Discover your inner resources and build upon them. Let go of what is not helpful to you in order to allow room for inspiration. Feel deeply good about yourself, rather than bravado. Satisfy your real need rather than your fancies. Your picture of yourself should be that of a tree, deeply rooted in rich soil, branches among the stars. Hold to that in times of stress.

Sagittarius Sun/Gemini Moon

Not only do you seek knowledge and experience, you wish also to build from this a sense of meaning and a philosophy of life. Your instinct is always to find out more, to communicate and to be mentally stimulated, and you eternally balance this by an effort to find patterns and things worth believing in. This means that you can be clever and resourceful, for you look at things from such a variety of angles. You are likely to be a lively, chatty person with many friends and many skills. The one place where you may not look for inspiration and revelation is inside, at your own feelings and needs and, in fact, you may be using your mental skills to escape having to confront certain parts of yourself. Rest assured that all of you is lovable and acceptable, even if it may be irrational, childish, mundane or 'silly'. Sometimes the deepest truth is discovered in human closeness. Nourish your body and your emotions, as well as your mind, and don't reject parts of yourself as petty, stupid or unworthy. Give yourself periods of quiet, away from external stimuli, and take note of your dreams, for they may contain some helpful hints.

Sagittarius Sun/Cancer Moon

You have far more need of emotional closeness, rapport and affection than most people would guess, from looking at you. Instead of overtly seeking gratification and attention, you may instead cater to the needs of others. On the positive side this means you are extremely charitable and caring, an excellent host or hostess and a cheerful companion to all. On the negative side, it can mean that your own needs go a-begging, because you are continually hoping someone will get the message that what you are giving is what you want to receive – but no one picks up on this. Conversely, you may choose to behave in an irrational or unreliable fashion, secretly hoping someone will 'mother' you (though possibly you won't admit this even to yourself). You may be unwilling to recognise your possessiveness, philosophising and rationalising to hide it, and this can make loving you an unrewarding job, for you may not give loved ones the satisfaction of knowing they are needed! On the positive side, you are an imaginative, intuitive person, well able to understand human issues and to express compassion in a way that gets results. You can be creative and dramatic, drawing upon an inner well of wisdom. Look inside, at what you really want, and have the honesty to make sure you get it!

Sagittarius Sun / Leo Moon

You are a great playgirl or playboy. Somewhere, deep inside, you have the conviction that you bear a charmed life, and because of this your life can, at times, appear to take on a magical quality, where people say 'How did you manage to pull *that* off?!' Self-belief is the trick, of course. However, the 'down' side of looking towards the light and bright can be that you sometimes miss what's in the shadows, and this can make for a 'Polyanna' attitude that isn't productive in the long run because it makes you less realistic. You need lots of attention – in fact you may feel worthwhile and 'real' only when you occupy the centre of the stage. Thus, you may be able to give of your warmth and love only to those whom you feel love and admire you. Learn to love yourself for what you truly are and then your companions can be chosen from people who will give you sincere support, rather than mere cheerleaders. If you come from a place of inner security, then you really can move mountains!

Sagittarius Sun / Virgo Moon

Sometimes you get on your own nerves. Just when you are set to charge off after some wonderful scheme, something inside you says 'Did you close the window? Have you cleaned your teeth? And have you checked out all the small print, because you know you are sure to have missed something'. This can be monumentally frustrating, a recipe for anxiety and futility, or it can mean a person who, while accomplishing less than you would like, possesses both breadth of vision and eye for detail, producing results that are inspiring and workable. You cannot possibly be perfect in every detail, so learn to compromise and delegate and use your powers of discrimination to decide where precision is essential, and where it would be an indulgence. Move between the general and the particular in an aware fashion, rather than being pushed from pillar to post by worries. No one can be perfect in everything, and that's a stone-cold fact, so value yourself, short-comings and all. Sort yourself out – lovingly – rather than seeking to sort out the world, then you may become as capable as even *your* heart could desire.

Sagittarius Sun / Libra Moon

By being indestructibly cheerful, enthusiastic and positive you seek to be a desirable companion and so ensure that you have the companions you wish for. You have a deep love of philosophy, peace and the beauty of concepts, and you seek people with whom to share this. You can be dreamy and idealistic, and while you need periods of calm and solitude you do not like to be truly alone – life is so much more fun with someone to share it. You don't like discord, and will reason yourself out of your feelings and needs rather than face this. Learn to experience your own needs rather than escaping into philosophy, or moralising. The heart has its own laws. Respect these – it does not mean you will be 'uncivilised'. Sometimes discord may have to be braved in the cause of a more soundly-based relationship. Remember 'beauty is truth'. You have the skills to restore harmony, which can then achieve greater depth. Don't short change yourself by over-compromise. You have the instincts of a diplomat and tactician and the heart of an explorer and opportunist, so the world can be your oyster. Regularly treat yourself to what uplifts your spirit and soothes your soul.

Sagittarius Sun/Scorpio Moon

Outwardly you may bounce around like Tigger but you hide a dark and private heart. Your intense passions and possessive instincts are at variance with your positive, humourous exterior, and so it is hard for you to get what you want, for you so rarely declare yourself. Frustration and inner pain may cause your philosophical breadth to narrow to cynicism. You may feel that your heart's desire never materialises, without seeing that your suspicious reactions and lack of commitment are precluding this. While maintaining your own freedom you may seek to bind others tightly, and lack of trust or acknowledgement of your own needs can make relationships with you difficult. However, it certainly does not have to be this way. You have the gift of both scope of vision and depth of experience, so you can be one of the most wise, powerful and giving of people if you so choose. Do not blame others. Resist compulsive control of situations and people. Have the courage to look inwards, to possess yourself, direct your passions and encompass your own needs in the scheme of things – do not expect others to satisfy all of these. Your richness of experience, your passion and your beliefs can combine to form an individual of warmth, magnetism, idealism and effectuality. Get your team of horses under control, and believe in love.

Appendix 2

ZODIACAL COMPATIBILITY

To assess fully the compatibility of two people the astrologer needs to have the entire chart of each individual, and while Sun-sign factors will be noticeable, there is a legion of other important points to be taken into account. Venus and Mercury are always very close to the Sun, and while these are often in the Sun sign, so intensifying its effect, they may also fall in one of the signs lying on either side of your Sun sign. So, as a 'Sagittarius' you may have Venus and/or Mercury in Scorpio or Capricorn, and this will increase your empathy with these signs. In addition the Moon and all the other planets including the Ascendant and Midheaven need to be taken into account. So if you have always been drawn to Cancers, maybe you have Moon or Ascendant in Cancer.

In order to give a vivid character sketch things have to be stated graphically. You should look for the dynamics at work, rather than be too literal about interpretation – for instance, you may find that you have no problem with Taureans, but you may be aware of strong contrasts in your approaches. It is up to the two of you whether a relationship works, for it can if you are both committed. Part of that is using the awareness you have to help, not necessarily as a reason for abandoning the relationship. There are always points of compatibility, and we are here to learn from each other.

On a scale of 1 (worst) to 4 (best), here is a table to assess instantly the superficial compatibility rating between Sagittarius and companions:

Sagittarius 3	Gemini 3
Capricorn 2	Cancer 1
Aquarius 4	Leo 4
Pisces 1	Virgo 2
Aries 4	Libra 3
Taurus 1	Scorpio 2

SAGITTARIUS COMPATIBILITIES

Sagittarius with Sagittarius

Two centaurs galloping together may throw up so much dust that they can hardly see each other! Neither may mind this too much, as long as the partner doesn't get in the way! This may not make for a particularly intimate relationship, but that may not be important to either of you, as long as you are heading for the same points on that far horizon. Two Saggitarians can bear out the description of the image – that love is not so much two people gazing at each other, but gazing ahead, at some shared ideal or objective – an inspiring thought.

As lovers Enthusiasm may be in plentiful supply, but your encounters may be confined largely to notes pinned to the fridge, unless you both slow up. Ms Sagittarius feels at home with this enterprising character who answers so much that is inside her, while Mr Sagittarius is drawn to this woman who seems – at last – to respect his freedom. However, in the long run he may find that 'freedom' isn't quite so wonderful when freely given, and he may wish someone would keep the homefires burning and give him something to bolt at. She, in turn, may secretly wish for more intimacy, and as women are often more realistic about their feelings, that is what she may seek. Also Ms Sagittarius will express resentment loudly if she is left literally 'holding the baby'. This relationship either works pretty well, or not at all.

As friends Even Saggitarian lovers are primarily friends, and it is satisfying to have someone to share one's sense of adventure, scope of vision and philosophies. You may argue about morals and beliefs, for each knows best!

As business partners Your chariot is heading hell-for-leather towards the cliff edge unless you get sound monetary advice. Each of you has loads of ideas and energy, so good in that respect. Avoid arguing!

Sagittarius with Capricorn

Capricorn can satisfy Sagittarius's need to have something to strain against and escape from! It always seems as if cautious Capricorn is pulling in the reins. However, Fire and Earth often have a strong attraction, and Sagittarius often senses that Capricorn is going somewhere, albeit much too slowly, and can cope with things that Sagittarius finds intolerable, like money, routines and traffic regulations. With a little patience this can work well, as you complement each other.

As lovers Sexual attraction may be strong. Sagittarian exuberance and optimism are a real tonic to Capricorn, who may be gloomy at times, while Sagittarius appreciates the reliable presence of the Goat. Capricorn, last of the Earth signs, often possesses a covert idealism and longing for the magical, which Sagittarius can embody, while 'I'm-up-for-anything' Sagittarius is secretly terrified of practical details which Capricorn manages so perfectly. Ms Sagittarius admires the rock-like quality of the Goat and his restrained sensuality, while Mr Sagittarius is drawn to the quiet magnetism of this self-assured female. Of course, Sagittarius may get fed up with what he or she may call Capricorn's negativity, while Capricorn's patience may be stretched by Sagittarian unreliability and inconsistency. Work at it and remember what first attracted you.

As friends Sagittarian schemes sometimes founder on the rocks of cold, hard facts, and while they pretend not to care, secretly they do. Capricorn can give form and substance, so Sagittarius achieves more even than envisioned. Respect each other, value the differences between you.

As business partners This can work excellently if Sagittarius will accept that Capricorn really does understand money, and should be listened to, and if Capricorn will value Sagittarian initiative and exuberance.

Sagittarius with Aquarius

Both of you are freedom freaks, and things should go well, as neither makes demands on the other. You find each other interesting, and there may be long discussions about ideas, plans and visions. Sagittarius may find Aquarius a little stubborn, but will simply go round him or her and each is prone to take the moral high ground. However, both are capable of shrugging shoulders and forgetting about it – usually.

As lovers There is much that attracts you, but unless there are some good Moon/Mars/Venus contacts it is unlikely to be sexual passion. Yes, you will get along fine, although Aquarius may prove a little too cool and detached for fiery Sagittarius. Ms Sagittarius finds this individualist very magnetic, while Mr Sagittarius is drawn to independent Ms Aquarius. Trouble can arise when the share of freedom isn't quite equal – which it can rarely be – and this can give rise to arguments, especially if there are children. It is likely that true intimacy and closeness will be lacking. You may both be quite happy with this, but there is always the chance that something more challenging and emotionally demanding could knock one of you out of your crystal sphere.

As friends Friendship really is the keynote of this duo, and it is an aspect that you will both value deeply. There may be many shared interests in offbeat, exotic or adventurous subjects, lots of projects and possibly a lively circle of friends. You could share a bohemian 'open house' with friends coming in at the back door, borrowing books, swapping magazines and arranging impromptu get-togethers.

As business partners Some Aquarians are realistic and practical, in which case, fine. If not, make sure your castles in the air have foundations.

Sagittarius and Pisces

Because the 'old' ruler of Pisces was Jupiter, shared with Sagittarius, these two can have points of contact. Both are idealistic, philosophical and somewhat otherworldly. However, Sagittarius is too insensitive for Pisces, and Pisces frustrates Sagittarius by being beyond even the Archer's ken.

As lovers At first this can be a tale of ethereal romanticism. Pisces seems to answer all the Sagittarian ideals, while Sagittarius offers a strength and heartiness that makes all Pisces' dreams seem possible. Ms Sagittarius is fascinated by this gentle, dreamy man, while Mr Sagittarius is bewitched by elusive Ms Pisces. However, after a while Pisces may feel deeply hurt by Sagittarian unreliability, and see that all the plans are built on shifting sand, while Sagittarius becomes impatient of Piscean moods. Sagittarius may, in the end, be outraged to find someone has been more unpredictable than themselves, as the Fish slips to balmier seas. To avoid considerable hurt, Sagittarius needs to work on being considerate, tactful and reliable, at least on important matters, and Pisces needs to find emotional support elsewhere.

As friends Here the best may come out of the partnership, for Pisces gently deepens Sagittarian awareness and injects subtlety, while Sagittarius galvanises Pisces. Joint schemes and dreams may forge a close bond, with giggles as an added bonus.

As business partners Unless you both have a hefty dollop of Earth in your respective charts, this is likely to end in shipwreck. Pisces only inflates Sagittarius's bubble, until it obscures all common sense and bursts under its own tension, and everyone catches cold. Both can then feel let down and blame each other. You have some brilliant ideas – get sound, practical and financial guidance.

Sagittarius with Aries

This is an exuberant combination of playmates and comrades-in-arms. Sagittarius can at times be just a little patronising towards Aries, whom he or she may see as childishly, but delightfully impulsive. However, Sagittarius isn't one to put a damper on anything, least of all Aries, and the two may forage far and wide in search of challenge and excitement. Trouble is, who will tend the hearth? Neither may feel this is important, until it gets cold and dark and they want supper . . .

As lovers All sound and fury at the start, with sexual experimentation and ardent expression. Ms Sagittarius is excited by the energy and verve of Mr Aries, and Mr Sagittarius feels he has found a woman who can answer his zest for life. Neither is that sensitive. It is possible that your partnership could be quite casual, although that may not answer your need for romance. There could be some spectacular rows, but as neither bears a grudge you could pick up the crockery together quite amicably. However, Aries may be a little jealous and demanding for the Archer's taste, and Sagittarian insistence on freedom could put a strain even on this jolly duo. Work at understanding and restraint.

As friends You have loads in common and should have adventures of all sorts together. You may enjoy competing, intellectually, verbally or in sport, and you should share a love of exploring, even on the most mundane level of swapping exotic recipes or sampling different beers until someone ends up under the table. But not all Sagittarians and Ariens are noisy extraverts, by any means, and many will enjoy quieter pursuits.

As business partners Someone needs to hold the reins firmly and you may both be too hell-bent on tearing off at the horizon even to think of restraint. Someone needs to manage the money and schedules.

Sagittarius with Taurus

You two are like chalk and cheese, one orientated towards comfort, security and stability, the other seeking expansion, adventure and the magic of the possible. Because of this, like all Fire/Earth combinations, there may be much fascination especially at the start.

As lovers Sexual attraction may be very strong at first. Ms Sagittarius thinks she has never seen such an assured, powerful male, while Mr Sagittarius is knocked off his heels by the sensual ambience of Ms Taurus. It seems to Sagittarius that Taurus has uncovered a treasure trove that has eluded all her or his rainbow chasing. Sagittarius is ardent and romantic while Taurus is sensuous – Taurus shows Sagittarius how to ground and express passion, while Sagittarius is very exciting to Taurus, so at first sex may be quite wild. Secretly Taurus may feel that sooner or later Sagittarius will 'see sense', but instead Sagittarius sees red when Taurus makes them miss the bus yet again. Sagittarius may leave the door banging on its hinges, while Taurus takes the cheque book. For this to work, keep your sense of wonder and be prepared to make very big compromises. You could find it is worth it.

As friends If you do strike up a friendship you may be endlessly amused and bemused by the other, quite convinced you are in the presence of someone from another planet. Taurus can give foundation to Sagittarian schemes, and Sagittarius can galvanise Taurus, if you will let each other near.

As business partners If you can get this to work it can be excellent, for you are each what the other needs. Taurus has the common sense and money sense; Sagittarius has all the enthusiasm and enterprise any organisation could need. Maintain respect for each other and have separate areas. Sagittarius is a good salesperson and entrepreneur; Taurus is a planner.

Sagittarius with Gemini

This can work well if there are shared interests, otherwise the danger is that you could both perpetually find yourselves at opposite ends of the country. There should be a relationship here somewhere, but each of you is too busy chasing deals and dreams to think much about it – and *think* is the operative word. There may not be much emotion in this partnership, unless you have some planets in Water signs. You can be great mates and keep each other interested, although Sagittarius may wish for greater warmth and become uncharacteristically demanding.

As lovers You will find each other very attractive at first, because you each offer the variety the other craves, and it may be possible to keep up the excitement for a long time. Ms Sagittarius responds to this man's delicious, wicked wit, and Mr Sagittarius realises that here is a lady who can make him really think, as well as more exotic things, in Jupiterian tradition. Neither of you will think anything of driving all day and night for some special attraction, and if you get married this could be celebrated (and indeed consummated!) at the top of the Empire State Building, in a submarine or a horse-drawn caravan. Neither of you takes well to boredom or routine. In time, however, Sagittarius may find there isn't enough substance to Gemini and – wait for it! – may wish for more commitment!

As friends Gemini can poke fun at Sagittarius so entertainingly that the Archer's robust ego remains intact. And Gemini provides so many ideas for Sagittarius to turn into philosophy. You could have fun hunting down the trendiest spots or making some of your own. Never a dull moment.

As business partners The fire-crackers could turn to Will-o'-the-Wisps unless you get good financial advice and support, and do some planning.

Sagittarius with Cancer

Sagittarius finds it very hard to endure Cancerian moods, let alone understand them. This is one of the most unpromising combinations, because Cancer deeply needs security and is painfully sensitive, while the Archer has hobnail boots that were made for walking – and seemingly trampling – crustacean claws. However, you have much to offer each other, and if you are prepared to work very hard this relationship could go the distance and expand you both at the same time – in fact, if it lasts you *will* expand, believe me!

As lovers Magnetic at first. Ms Sagittarius knows there is more to this inscrutable man than meets the eye and longs to draw him out, while Mr Sagittarius finds Ms Cancer fascinating and sexy. However, sexually the Ice Age may set in on Sagittarian gaffs. Sagittarius, puzzled and irritated, threshes about, deeper and deeper into the mire: 'I never said your mother was an old bag. She's just one of the old school, prudish, authoritarian, always right. There's nothing wrong with that – it's the spirit that built the Empire. If you want an empire that is, if you think it's morally defensible . . .' Cancer needs to realise that whatever views Sagittarius expresses the love between them is real and enduring, and Sagittarius needs to . . . well . . . learn some sensitivity. That's all there is to it.

As friends One thing you can share is a love of the good things of life, such as food, wine and opulent comfort. Sagittarius can show Cancer some laughs, while Cancer can deepen Sagittarian appreciation, slowing them to subtler pleasures. There is a respect for tradition in Sagittarians – tradition that enhances their status or serves their ends, that is – that can find resonance with Cancer.

As business partners Can be really good. You will need separate areas and Sagittarius must tolerate Cancerian thrift and caution.

Sagittarius with Leo

These two get along very well, especially at first. Both are playful and have enormous faith in life and themselves. There may sometimes be a struggle for the position of top dog, and Leo may find that Sagittarius, despite all the fine words, doesn't quite come up with the required commitment, thus making the Lion very jealous. Neither of you likes the dirty work – this relationship works best if you can afford servants, or at the very least a home help!

As lovers Lots of fire and passion, probably with some spectacular rows and reunions. Ms Sagittarius is drawn to this big-hearted guy, while Mr Sagittarius recognises that here is a woman who can encompass all his dreams and schemes. This relationship can fly high on fantasy, but the plain old facts that bedevil everyone wait at the airport for Leo and Sagittarius, too. You could feel disappointed with each other, when what you are really disappointed with is life. Keep your dreams aloft and don't expect too much of each other. Despite all you have in common you may need to work at empathy and understanding, but you may revel in your image of two 'beautiful people' with neon-bright pizzazz.

As friends Naturally you will get on very well as friends. Sagittarius is a-crackle with ideas for excursions, holidays and such like, while Leo enjoys them and boasts about them afterwards. Sometimes Sagittarius feels impelled to take Leo down a peg and both assume the god-given right to have their own way, but as neither is oversensitive they may each feel comfortable with a perpetual power struggle. After all, it makes life interesting.

As business partners You could fly sky-high on hot air and then find there is no safety net. Your plans are no doubt stylish and inventive. Carry the best of them through and get sound backing.

Sagittarius with Virgo

Whoever said that 'you can dodge an elephant but not a gnat' could have been talking about a Virgo–Sagittarius partnership. Sagittarius finds there are things that Virgo presents that somehow cannot be escaped, however much they sting, while Virgo may simply circumvent Sagittarian excesses – albeit very anxiously! Although wild and wonderful Sagittarius leaves for the stratosphere while Virgo is still searching for the needle in the haystack, Sagittarius has to come back down – and Virgo *finds* the needle! The two of you could wind each other up to a pitch of agitation on Virgo's part, and frustration on Sagittarius's. However, it doesn't *have* to be like that . . .

As lovers Sexual attraction is often intense between this Fire and Earth sign. Ms Sagittarius is intrigued by Mr Cool Virgo, and Mr Sagittarius is hot in pursuit of this restrained and subtly sensuous woman. Sagittarius often feels tied down by Virgo, and yet there is something inescapable about these ties. Virgo always has a sound reason for requests and may awaken the Sagittarian's dormant sense of duty. In addition, the secret sexual doubts that Sagittarius nourishes may seem irrelevant in the face of Virgoan pragmatism. Life can be hell as Virgo tidies and sorts and Sagittarius scatters. However, there is likely to be considerable intellectual rapport here and each may find the other throws unexpected light on matters.

As friends Each of you is curious about life and while Virgo searches for proofs, Sagittarius is sniffing the wind for clues and possibilities, so each of you finds your version of the truth. Here there is much to complement and argue about – and to be honest, Sagittarius is only too pleased to leave the planning to someone else.

As business partners Great if you each have your own niche, dire if you're forced together. Virgo must trim Sagittarian proposals down to size and make them work, without destroying them, and Sagittarius simply cannot always have it his or her way.

Sagittarius with Libra

Libra has a very strong sense of relationship as something that is greater than the sum of its parts, and this could just appeal to Sagittarian idealism as long as it doesn't mean that freedom is compromised. Libra is tolerant enough to cope with most things, and sufficiently couple-orientated to stop the partnership dissipating as the good times roll. Each knows how to enjoy life, although Libra is a little less raucous, and Sagittarius may accuse Libra of 'posing'. However, many Sagittarians love to be up with the latest trend, and Libra can show the way to do this in convincing style.

As lovers All rainbows and romance. Ms Sagittarius turns all dreamy under the gaze of this smooth charmer, while Mr Sagittarius likes a 'gal who knows what it means to be a gal'. He is even more enthusiastic when he finds there is a sharp mind under the soft tresses. This can be a 'marriage of true minds' or a couple of good-time Harrys treating life as a ball. Communication is good, but may break down when Libra is still in the bathroom and Sagittarius is stamping on the doorstep, coat over arm. However, if anyone can teach Sagittarius a little consideration it is Libra. Depth and commitment may run thin at times, yet these two may still hold hands and watch the stars in the geriatric ward.

As friends Both of you like company, usually, and you may be part of a trendy and sophisticated crowd. Or you may prefer more thoughtful pursuits, or rambles together where Libra looks at the flowers and Sagittarius watches the clouds. Things work best if Sagittarius shows just a little restraint and Libra can drop the genteel air – or at least not mind when Sagittarius takes the Mickey!

As business partners You both create your own luck, and you will need it if your enterprise is to be more than a flashy shopfront. To fill the warehouse and the coffers get some down-to-earth support.

Sagittarius with Scorpio

The one thing you have in common is that you are people of extremes – Scorpio's intensity is matched by Sagittarian ardour. Unfortunately, Scorpionic possessiveness and jealousy is equally matched by Sagittarian unreliability and insistence on an open back door to the relationship. For Scorpio this is far too draughty, and the resulting manipulations can enrage Sagittarius if he or she notices!

As lovers Because the sexual side may be very exciting, Scorpio may decide that access to the loins is fine as long as the door to the heart is barricaded. Ms Sagittarius's love of danger is aroused by this man, and she longs to take the lid off the pressure cooker, while Mr Sagittarius may throw all caution to the wind in pursuit of this seductress. In the long run Sagittarius cannot hope to cope with Scorpionic manipulation and may become confused and angry – and absent. Coming back with a bouquet and a grin won't win any prizes, because by now Scorpio has read and memorised every tell-tale receipt and cryptic scrawl in the diary. For this to work Sagittarius needs to take time out to explain, and apologise, and Scorpio needs to have faith in Sagittarian candour, and in his or her own ability to see straight through the Archer's naive deceptions.

As friends Scorpio can appreciate Sagittarian cheerfulness, while Sagittarius may be intrigued by the way Scorpio seems to look at the underbelly of life. Sagittarius may feel it's worth hanging around in the crypt if something interesting is going to show up. The more philosophical 'awakened' type of Sagittarius can find much to fascinate and absorb in Scorpio.

As business partners This can work really well, for Sagittarius makes the deals while Scorpio scours the small print for drawbacks. Scorpio is usually much better with money, but should take care not to dampen all the Sagittarian enthusiasm.

Appendix 3

TRADITIONAL ASSOCIATIONS AND TOTEM

Each sign of the zodiac is said to have an affinity with certain colours, plants, stones and other substances. Of course, we cannot be definite about this, for not only do sources vary regarding specific correspondences – we also have the rest of the astrological chart to bear in mind. Some people also believe that the whole concept of such associations is invalid. However, there certainly do seem to be some links between the character of each of the signs and the properties of certain substances. It is up to you to experiment and to see what works for you.

Anything that traditionally links with Sagittarius is likely to intensify Sagittarian traits. So if you wish, for some reason, to be cautious and restrained, you should steer clear of the colour purple and sage and frankincense essential oils! However, if you want to be your Sagittarian, adventurous best, it may help to surround yourself with the right stimuli, especially on a down day. Here are some suggestions:

- **Colours** Mauve, violet, royal purple, indigo, rich blue, possibly some deep reds.
- **Flowers** Carnation, honeysuckle, rose.

- **Metal** Tin. Many Sagittarians will like to wear gold, however.
- **Stones** Amethyst, sugilite, lepidolite.

Aromatherapy

Aromatherapy uses the healing power of essential oils both to prevent ill health and to maintain good health. Specific oils can sometimes be used to treat specific ailments. Essential oils are concentrated and powerful substances, and should be treated with respect. Buy from a reputable source. *Do not use any oil in pregnancy* until you have checked with a reputable source that it is okay (see 'Further Reading'). *Do not ingest oils* – they act through the subtle medium of smell, and are absorbed in massage. *Do not place undiluted on the skin.* For massage: Dilute in a carrier oil such as sweet almond or grapeseed, two drops of oil to one teaspoon of carrier. Use in an oil burner, six to ten drops at a time, to fragrance your living area.

Essential oils

- **Clove** Warm and spicy, associated with baked apples and Christmas (or, by some, with the dentist!). A good stimulant, relieving fatigue. May relieve toothache, when applied straight to the cavity. Analgesic and antiseptic, good for combatting digestive and respiratory infections and sore throats.
- **Frankincense** Rich and majestic, this oil promotes spirituality. It is also good for stress and respiratory problems.
- **Sage** Great general tonic, useful especially in convalescence, or simply when you feel worn out. Helpful for relieving menstruation and menopause problems.

Naturally you are not restricted to oils ruled by your sign, for in many cases treatment by other oils will be beneficial, and you should consult a qualified aromatherapist for advice if you have a particular problem. If a problem persists, consult your GP.

Your birth totem

According to the tradition of certain native North American tribes, each of the signs of the zodiac is known by a totem animal. The idea of the totem animal is useful, for animals are powerful, living symbols and they can do much to put us in touch with our potentials. Knowing your totem animal is different from knowing your sign, for your sign is used to define and describe you – as we have been doing in this book – whereas your totem shows you a path of potential learning and growth.

The totem for Sagittarius is the Owl, and you also have an affinity with Grizzly Bear and Hawk. You were born in the Long Nights Time. There is a difficulty here, for the North American lore is based on the seasonal cycle. Thus for those of you living in the Southern Hemisphere, it may be worth bearing in mind the totems of your opposite, Gemini. These are Deer, also Eagle and possibly Butterfly, the Air totem, and the Gemini time is called Flowering Time.

Owl, the night hunter, possesses almost uncanny abilities that help in the tracking down of prey. The Owl is often a symbol for wisdom, linked to the goddess Athene and to the 'flower-faced' Welsh goddess, Blodeuwedd. Made from flowers, she is connected to the total 'knowingness' of nature. Owl brings deep insight, and can be a powerful ally in those seeking to expand consciousness. Its soundless flight is synonymous with Sagittarian inner journeys, and its hunting skill denotes the ability of Sagittarius to be adventurous and well aimed in endeavours.

Contacting your totem

You can use visualisation techniques to make contact with the energies of your birth totem. You will need to be very quiet, still and relaxed. Make sure you won't be disturbed. Have a picture of your totem before you, and perhaps burn one of the oils we have mentioned, in an oil burner, to intensify the atmosphere. When you are ready close your eyes and imagine that you are your totem animal – imagine how it feels, what it smells, sees, hears. What are its feelings, instincts and abilities? Keep this up for as long as you are comfortable, then come back to everyday awareness. Write down your experiences and eat or drink something to ground you. This can be a wonderfully refreshing and mind-clearing exercise, and you may find it inspiring. Naturally, if you feel you have other totem animals – creatures with which you feel an affinity – you are welcome to visualise these. Look out for your totems in the wild – there may be a message for you.

Further reading and resources

Astrology for Lovers, Liz Greene, Unwin, 1986. The title may be misleading, for this is a serious, yet entertaining and wickedly accurate account of the signs. A table is included to help you find your Rising Sign. This book is highly recommended.

Teach Yourself Astrology, Jeff Mayo and Christine Ramsdale, Hodder & Stoughton, 1996. A classic textbook for both beginner and practising astrologer, giving a fresh insight to birth charts through a unique system of personality interpretation.

Love Signs for Beginners, Kristyna Arcarti, Hodder & Stoughton, 1995. A practical introduction to the astrology of romantic relationships, explaining the different roles played by each of the planets and focussing particularly on the position of the Moon at the time of birth.

Star Signs for Beginners, Kristyna Arcarti, Hodder & Stoughton, 1993. An analysis of each of the star signs – a handy, quick reference.

The Moon and You for Beginners, Teresa Moorey, Hodder & Stoughton, 1996. Discover how the phase of the Moon when you were born affects your personality. This book looks at the nine lunar types – how they live, love, work and play, and provides simple tables to enable you to find out your birth phase and which type you are.

The New Compleat Astrologer, Derek and Julia Parker, Mitchell Beazley, 1984. This is a complete introduction to astrology with instructions on chart calculation and planetary tables, as well as clear and interesting descriptions of planets and signs. Including history and reviewing present-day astrology, this is an extensive work, in glossy, hardback form, with colour illustrations.

The Knot of Time: Astrology and the Female Experience, Lindsay River and Sally Gillespie. For personal growth, from a gently feminine perspective, this book has much wisdom.

The Astrology of Self-discovery, Tracy Marks, CRCS Publications, 1985. This book is especially useful for Moon signs.

The Astrologer's Handbook, Francis Sakoian and Louis Acker, Penguin, 1984. This book explains chart calculation and takes the reader through the meanings of signs and planets, with extensive interpretations of planets in signs and houses. In addition, all the major aspects between planets and angles are interpreted individually. A very useful work.

Aromatherapy for Pregnancy and Childbirth, Margaret Fawcett RGN, RM, LLSA, Element, 1993.

The Aromatherapy Handbook, Daniel Ryman, C W Daniel, 1990.

Useful addresses

The Faculty of Astrological Studies

The claim of the Faculty to provide the 'finest and most comprehensive astrological tuition in the world' is well founded. Correspondence courses of a high calibre are offered, leading to the internationally recognised diploma. Evening classes, seminars and summer schools are taught, catering for the complete beginner to the most experienced astrologer. A list of trained consultants can be supplied on request, if you wish for a chart interpretation. For further details telephone (UK code) 0171 700 3556 (24-hour answering service); or fax 0171 700 6479. Alternatively, you can write, with SAE, to: Ref. T. Moorey, FAS., BM7470, London WC1N 3XX, UK.

Educational

California Institute of Integral Studies, 765 Ashbury St, San Francisco, CA 94117. Tel: (415) 753-6100

Kepler College of Astrological Arts and Sciences, 4518 University Way, NE, Suite 213, Seattle, WA 98105. Tel: (206) 633-4907

Robin Armstrong School of Astrology, Box 5265, Station 'A', Toronto, Ontario, M5W 1N5, Canada. Tel: (416) 923-7827

Vancouver Astrology School, Astraea Astrology, Suite 412, 2150 W Broadway, Vancouver, V6K 4L9, Canada. Tel: (604) 536-3880

The Southern Cross Academy of Astrology, PO Box 781147, Sandton, SA 2146 (South Africa) Tel: 11-468-1157; Fax: 11-468-1522

Periodicals

American Astrology Magazine, PO Box 140713, Staten Island, NY 10314-0713. e-mail: am.astrology@genie.gies,com

The Journal of the Seasons, PO Box 5266, Wellesley St, Auckland 1, New Zealand. Tel/fax: (0)9-410-8416

The Federation of Australian Astrologers Bulletin, PO Box 159, Stepney, SA 5069. Tel/fax: 8-331-3057

Aspects, PO Box 2968, Rivonia, SA 2128, (South Africa)
Tel: 11-864-1436

Realta, The Journal of the Irish Astrological Association, 4 Quay Street, Galway, Ireland. Available from IAA, 193, Lwr Rathmines Rd, Dublin 6, Ireland.

Astrological Association, 396 Caledonian Road, London, N1 1DN. Tel: (UK code) 0171 700 3746; Fax: 0171 700 6479. Bi-monthly journal issued.